MOTHERS
OUGHT TO UTTER
ONLY NICETIES

MOTHERS
OUGHT TO UTTER
ONLY NICETIES

KJ Hannah Greenberg

UNBOUND
CONTENT
Englewood, NJ

ISBN 978-1-936373-54-3
Cover art: © 2017 KJ Hannah Greenberg
Cover and interior design: © 2017 Dana Martin
Author photo: © 2017 Yiftach Paltrowitz
Published in the United States by Unbound Content, LLC,
Englewood, NJ.
The poems in this collection are all original and previously
unpublished with the exception of those listed in the credits
page at the end of the volume.

MOTHERS OUGHT TO UTTER ONLY NICETIES
First edition 2017

UNBOUND
CONTENT

Contents

Part Two
Parenting Ourselves

Preface

New beginnings are at once arduous and revealing. In nascent life, we find truth's viscera-impacted glory. Whether we seek to fashion children or other, lesser products, such as texts, their complexities profoundly alter us. That is, whether we birth the next generation of people or we birth assemblages of words, we open ourselves to unlimited marvels, including, and especially, personal discovery. It's good for us to let cells mingle and multiply and for us to allow our ruminations to amalgamate and repurpose us. It's correspondingly beneficial to read about such goings on in volumes such as *Mothers Ought to Utter Only Niceties.*

In this collection, "Part One: Parenting Our Dear Ones" makes manifold references to raising young. From overflowing diapers to adolescent dilemmas, from intersibling sauciness to surrendered careers, this section explores: The joy of discovering progeny emerging as "lawyers," "environmentalists," "bankers," and "clerics," all *before* naptime; the worry that some of those same sons and daughters might aspire (gasp!) to become writers; and the small consequences that result from years of being peed on, spit up upon, and drooled over all during such "vocation negotiations." Accordingly, the poems in this portion validate the miracle of moms and dads who rarely yield to emotional meltdowns, dramatic accusations, or plain 'ol funk. We're due some recognition.

Similarly, in this book's "Part Two: Parenting Ourselves," numerous claims get espoused about how cultivating texts is like cultivating offspring. Akin to parenting, writing provides no guarantees, nearly always depletes us of resources, and yet, when we least expect it, brings us unplumbed insights. As is true of raising our children, developing our words culls, for us, amazing phenomena whether we are "successful" in our ministrations or "fail" in our attempts to touch the heavens. As is the case with parenting, writing pushes us to keep our passions in line even when we might otherwise sprout like fungi or blaze like rockets. As writers, we ought to be able to cash in on some amount of welcome.

So, in more than 120 earnest bites, *Mothers Ought to Utter Only Niceties* celebrates the vacillating universes of children and of writing, of parents and of writers. Both the ache to make babies and the ache to fashion our feelings on paper amass, for us, fresh syntheses about corporeal, spiritual, and blended peculiarities of life.

KJ Hannah Greenberg
Jerusalem, 2017

Introduction: The Warrior's Mother

The warrior's mother, all peacock attitude, prayers, plus Galil submachine gun,
Settles, frustrated, at an ersatz table built of wood and bone; she loathes the enemy.
Euphony, as Mama knows, means cries, screams, railing in the night, sounding off,
Those others intend, insidiously, to kill her boys. Mama deploys, accordingly,
subversions.

She dreams, as well, of questionable warfare, of not limiting herself,
Of employing mobile extermination squads, poison gases, infectious diseases,
Random acts of pillaging, and unpredictable executions of POWs,
But bad characters, those who harbor lice, plague, attitude, wash up the media.

So, when tired from envisaging the offing of bandits, from imagining the flaying
of malevolents,
Mama dabs her forehead with cloth, adjusts her kerchief, rubs on lipstick, smiles
pretty;
News bureaus obfuscate in line with evil's agenda. Witnesses hide black,
disproportionate force,
Indiscriminate rocket attacks, the use of white phosphorous, most iniquities wrought
by "them."

That side's creation of orphans, disregard of appendages, illicit building, gall, sells
popcorn.
As such, foreign lies, depravation, tank shells full of depleted uranium, knife attacks,
Exaggerated accounts, retouched pictures, castrations of truth, yet sever maternal
conveyances.
Those nefarious actions bring Mama to knees of weariness, until they awaken
her martial heart.

Part One

Parenting Our Dear Ones

Charif
Mamas

There's a Seam

There's a seam
Of flesh, where her cheeks
Meet my breast. The balance
Is eyelids and pink fingers.
In her bath, I recall not
Red boats nor rubber ducks, but
How birth fictions once filled me.

There's a seam
At mitten's end, where her hands
Hold my hands. The plan
Is cruising in short flights.
At night, I wonder not
Soft lambs nor happy pups, but
On affection's sanity.

There's a seam
Inside, where her needs
Wave my dreams. The child
Is meant to recreate us.
When I pray, I hunger not
Grand roles and fancy schemes, but
Thank Perfection's gift to me.

The Zebra Hoof Beats of Buttercup Boys

Such small, flax heads
Wibbly lips, quivering
Past flaccid breasts' heated,
Nurturing white wonder.

Soft, pulsing basset ears,
So often overstepped extensions,
Reference spans since passed,
(Or visited infrequently).

My empty womb grows morning hopes,
My dreams sustained your belly kicks
While all those hiccupy coughs once stretched
My walls toward young new life.

Nutritional Inconveniences

My baby ate oat cakes.
My mother heart hurt more than my stomach.
Oat cakes and breast milk.
Lunch. For a child
With an unexpected visit to a play center.

Her baby ate rice.
Her mother heart hurt more than her stomach.
Rice and breast milk.
Dinner. For a child
With an unexpected passage through a war zone.

That baby ate sand.
That mother heart hurt more than her stomach.
Sand and breast milk.
Sustenance. For a child
With a life unexpectancy during a famine.

Alphabetical Trails

My baby leaves a trail
Of slime
-d-
Varmints.

My mollycoddle marks a route
Of toy
-d-
Words.

My cosset queen verbs a path
Of joy
-ful-
Xplorations.

My honey darling blazes directions
'til no
-one's-
The Yiser.

Baby Spits Peas

At three, baby spits peas
Across the dashboard, proving
She is woman rather than
Garbage can.

Shrugging, I pull
Tall boys toward
Quiet, against
Taller mouths.

I smile, shrugging away
Pain,
Residing in their futures.

Hummingbirds strung on wires won't
Waste time poised for flitting.
When needed, they dive
From hurt, hurrying
Rather than remaining.
Moving targets rarely die.

For Ezra:
Familial Wishes for a New Nighttime Traveler

Sleepy Buntling, Joyous Jumble,
Plucky Voyager, Baby Bumble,
Your Uncles magic up moonbeams.

Little Boykin, Sweet-faced Milkling,
Cotton Precious, Soft-kissed Silkling,
Your Aunties ease your tidal streams.

Grandpa's Cherished, Grandmas' Lambie,
Daddy's Darling, Mama's Fancy,
Your Family smooths your vessel's seams.

Small-voiced Sailor, Welcomed Wonder,
Wave-o-whisper! Cosmic thunder!
Our loving wraps around your seas.

My Daughter Bangs Pot Lids

My daughter bangs pot lids together--
Cymbals.
(Of) her growing independence.

She stalks our cats here--
There.
(Like) Sunny spots or dispositions.

Reaching Mommyward, she praises
Life.
(Is) good to me.

Simple Miracles

Slowly, a leaf falls,
From a giant tree.
Slowly, a wave rolls,
From a deeper sea.
Slowly, a cloud breaks,
Forms the darkest sky.
Slowly, a child learns,
Forms the question "why?"

Baby's Friends

Purple-pink ricochet laughter floats
By dirty laundry, opened envelopes,
Plus nappy coupons, 'long our halls,
After your sitter's been on call.

Tissue paper packages deck your shelves,
Where treasure bears smile among fabric selves.
Primary colored tubs pile by kitschy blocks,
Somebody's grandparents spoil you lots.

Then Auntie's doggies kiss you, jumping
Upon your minutiae, beyond your fumbling.
Floorward allies, they extend much praise,
For your nouveau, generous, highchair ways.

Waving, smiling, all gums, crawling,
Emphatically doorward; I capture you, small thralling.
Save you from glass, ensure your survival,
As you anticipate Daddy's arrival.

Little kingship, your empire's peopled fully
With subjects you can regularly bully.
Your snorts are cherished, your tweaks adored,
All's right with your actions; your minions applaud!

But Loving You

Little stones with twigs, what bits,
Trash perhaps, but laughing, you
Hand them to Mama.

Little chews or drips and sips,
Lunch to some, but smiling, you
Dine with Dad.

Little steps and words and joys,
Growth de rigueur, but loving you
Fills our lives.

Milk Moments

Go away little growl,
Little Guy demanded nursing,
Head held back, catching my light
In your growth of lips, cheeks, tongue.

My cups wash limpid, free of darkness,
As we share the wisdom of lactation,
Chaff's only culled as we pause for air
Or for lesser needs.

Then, during diaper changes,
Flickerings of serious poetics totter,
Coupling your vulnerable parameters,
With history more than nature.

Greater immolations,
You impecunious thief, come
When our mutual articulations
Sing home the moon.

Three Haikus for Childhood

Sylvan Song

The trees talk, too.
Theirs are wonderful legends
Regarding olden folk.

Friendship

Golden rays of hope,
Gleaming brightly, touching hearts,
Singing a loud "love!"

Mirage: Silent Flowers

Butterflies, en masse,
Are talking on the tree branches,
Creating a deceitful illusion

Parenting's Saxophone Smiles

When lads do play a piccolo, girls tweet upon a flute,
Bray through a brass trumpet or pluck sweet chords upon a lute,
Then blow a fife, yet sound a horn, and bang a drum, to boot;
Parenting gives me saxophone smiles.

Pellucid jars, small shiny things, some mother's pride, what's more,
Diaper bins, mâché birds on wing, plus blocks spilled on tiled floors,
Library books strewn all around, amongst stuffed beasts' mute roar;
Such bedlam makes me dance insanely.

Bright crayon wax, amongst our lumps of carrots, peas, potatoes,
My children's favorite meals make mounds on chairs, on rugs, on tables,
Nonetheless, I serve up more with gravy since I'm able;
Their messes inspire me to write.

Wee athletes, whom I'd emulate, one thousand years from now,
Leap over laundry, hesitate just to grab their towels,
Dear star-kissed heads nod in their bath, lull cradled on their boughs;
My offsprings' nap time can't come too soon.

Watching Raindrops Dance

We discover self-reference,
Between pieces of white bread,
To Divine incorporation.

School mornings, though,
Life's jobs completed on autopilot,
I often have to guess "hello."

The kids' return to "finding"
Themselves frequently elicits
My new moments,
Plus all the power of sleepy gray cats.

Cityscape perspectives yield
More that sparrow goings-on.
Sometimes, I can grasp able-bodied knowledge.

Natural Balance

In 1968, I drew; man
With two dots between his shoulders, and
A long stick between his legs.
Roy Kowitzsky gave woman two chest circles
Also, with dots.
The lunch monitor collected us and art.
Phone calls later, our
Parents disapproved. *National
Geographic* was removed
From Mrs. Kalback's second grade.

In 1991, I grew; breasts
With mother's milk between my shoulders, and
Feathered stretch marks between my legs.
My infant son cried for my chest circles
Also, with dots.
The shift waitress collected plates and poise.
Several courses later, my
Baby refreshed. Natural
Balance was restored
To Princeton's sandwich shop.

The Effect of Cumin on Mankind Can't Replace Pop-Pop

The effect of cumin on mankind
Wrought many anxious fathers-in-law;
Single-lens reflex camera were stymied
By the digital revolution.

For a Herculean moment,
Old collections of vinegared vials
Stopped working as medicine;
Purple pills replaced home remedies.

In a finger's snap, even autos
Seemed antiquated,
Compared to bullet trains
Or Concorde jets.

Yet, in our world's corner,
Toddlers' uneven steps
Continued to merit
Their Pop-Pop's hugs.

Daddy's Ankle Biters' Extravagance

My sister's hair color,
Her best friend's fashion,
Remain my puzzle.

Their toddlers' sheets, too,
Reek of pee, mornings
After thunder storms.

Contemporary mood disorders,
Like rain clouds, gather to
Suddenly drift home.

Such frozen ground covers
Omnipotence otherwise left over
As second-hand sunshine, in workers' barns.

When I rub my hand over my chest,
Feeling hair plus muscle,
That dose refreshes gaslight era contraptions.

Our older daughter bends in prayer,
Perched like a seed-deprived bird,
Glad for simple corn.

Sometimes, mindsets prove incompatible with infatuation.
Unsettled children might
Bite their pets' tails.

Then the Wind Brings: (An Elegiac Verse)

From brittle, broken leaves, those crackly bits of citrine memories,
Ambergel wisps of newborn hair, amuse bouche of life, materialized,
Quickly filled palaces assigned to lasses less vested than our principality's.

Hence her silvered flakes, faceward falling, complex, corded life, involved no
Binding. Our designee's kirtle failed, despite all, couldn't wholly ward off chilblains.
Swiftly, drugs, heralds, clerics were summoned, adamant to buoy her revised amnion.

Such embryonic buds stay sombulant, like geezers in old, overstuffed chairs,
For whom sun, humidity, heat, as well as oxygen hooked to chests, bring life,
Beckon support from doctors regarding "inguinal hernias," other "normal deviations."

Accordingly, select bottom-clothed nurslings, akin to elders, weigh in like colored
Stones. Chert, topaz, lapis. Their short life's an uncertain journey, twelve months at breast,
Sans professional redoubt, minus medical portcullises, exclusive of traditional protections.

Still, the pernicious will to live, to sift obvolute fluids, to strive, to conquer,
Evoking royal dreams of vanquishing quintessence privations, of thwarting
Trebuchets, of the worst kind, no matter how often those foes etch vulnerable pia mater.

Recall that agrarian groups would compensate their women, were wont to gift effort.
Moderns, unfortunately, ululate nothing for preemies' parents, tribute even less
Toward mother hearts whose promontories lay exposed, vestigial structures shattered.

When children stop breathing, we would benefit from segregating space, from temporalizing,
Wee aliquoted selves, their tiny sered limbs, trunks, faces, evermore. Those champions
Emerged opposed to fate, ran contrary to strictures for amputated food, drink, love.

Consider, that suppression by kin, plus newborn dependence, makes monsters of insouciant
Institutions of learning, Governance, deviant arts, sinister schadenfreude, each and every
Echo vitriolically among missed, "righteous" phalangy. Then, schooled men hide their ignominy.

Thereafter, life's salt rooms shed more than sweat. Forgetting takes days, years.
Sometimes, inhaled ions' powers fall short, counsel misspeaks, solace overlooks.
When wrapped in ushanka memories, it's tough to acknowledge fault.

So, medicos continue to task and tally daily, leaving would-be parents embracing bedtime
Retinues filled with lachrymose sighs, dyspeptic trances; childless milk, mislaid smiles.
Lambkins' portentous grasping, sleepless dreams, sweet burps, taste tart under the yaupons.

Bird Wonder

Feathery tufts beyond seed-filled bellies,
Flights of innocence toward the moon,
Where aerial summersaults sup, then rally
Fledglings from fragile nests too soon.

Realigned by light or shadow.
Transported, though sometimes quelled,
Measures past easy doubts' stumbling
Recall moments of love lived well.

Clouds coat old airstreams' essence,
Earth fires warm spiritual tunes.
Crystalline secrets again uncover
Heaven's sanction to flock and roam.

Among Seaweed

Flitting fishes,
Tangles green and gray,
Swim sky colors,
Slipping ocean to ocean.

Amid bone corals,
Anemones' rare beauty,
Brightly speckles certain,
Frugal graces.

Thick, heavy, pungent,
No land instrument can weigh
Sea gravity's
Capricious quality.

Loaded by stones,
Sunk, once treasured
Nigh alive. Nigh awake
Nigh replete.

G-d speed to others,
Among seaweed, small lips sigh.

Heart-Felt Festival

Bring gilded hunting horns of golden sound.
Strew flowers in the streets that surround.
Open straw baskets, replete with rare scents,
Light limitless lanterns; stake up some grand tents,
Build bonfires blazing, set caldrons warming,
Gather people; call my masses to swarm,
Announce my great honor, trumpet my grand joy,
This princess esteems her birth of a boy.

Formative
Growth

Education before Marriage (*a Cyhydedd Hir*)

Breakfast chatter brings
Wedding bells, does sing
Bright images.
I return your song,
For our dreams belong,
To tomorrow's child. Our strong
Ardor beats back time's edge.

Pomp and circumstance,
Prior to such romance,
Preceding our sweet chance
To realize hopes.
Books, great country miles,
Circumvent such style,
Should we choose to while
Away our days by rote.

Still, faith lends love great strength,
Endurance, spark, plus length,
Fidelity feeds truth's rank,
As a future befriended.
Two hearts twinned in promise,
We'll victor this distance,
Overcome the test,
Beloved, we'll transcend.

Vitreous Recollections: That Summer's Glaze

Familiar delight, miniature cyncephalus,
Who expertly sidestepped a butterfly-looking leaf,
Amidst further crunchy, colorful tree debris,
While scuffling new things underfoot, snapping their beauty
Beneath mighty, wee sandals such that entire worlds faded.

You were daughter mine. Small pluripotency,
Secret brinell, most ordinarily like a puff's caress, you
Toddled too low for rings hand over hand, struggled, instead,
To shimmy, in the wrong direction, on the fireman's pole.
Placated easily, though, by unfussy raita dribbled with honey.

Little sylph, petite sylvan spirit, baby girl, one that repudiated
Bedtime, save for bathy suds, mismatched bunnies, warm socks,
Frolicked in public fountains, around light posts, in sandboxes,
Then behind a rapidly pumping swing, from which
No sister, brother, other, or dog could salvage.

Accordingly, I refused customary gatekeepers' comforts, kisses,
So mistaken were their words, prayers, songs, deeds.
Sometimes, only a mother knows, feels so deeply
When a shoot's unnaturally pale, lethargic countenance
Summons up more ouchy tests then merely checking for anemia.

Modest dreamer, prodigious child, universe's host,
Whose stance spreads more yogic than preschool,
In my mind, privately, you're still attempting to smile
At pigeons, trying to help them jump full thunder
Into the splash pool's deepest end.

Holidays' Fallibility

My little girl,
Almost four, dies.
Foreign, fungus-like bodies
Spread beyond our doctors' control.

No transparent womb can,
Cradle against death;
We await that other part,
Existing unlike null or minus.

An asphyxiated fish,
She surfaces,
Neither calm nor crumpled;
Her misshapen body's elsewhere.

Elsewhere, cacophonic celebrants'
Trough-stuffed orifices
Greet parsimony with chilled cocktails.
Only my valise sentry sits threshold-ready.

Sparkling, crisis-packaged glitter,
Fills eyes and ears with rotten songs.
Slumping kitchenward, I dispose
Cherry port, anise, plus resin.

Sentiment drives hard on life's credenza.
While "pious" children sing,
"Eat, drink, spend."
I bid them drafts of grand "delight."

Song of Oenomelian

Balance carefully!

The stone stands clean in rain and time,
The river's dry, a spirit's find.
The dark clouds bring out hope and shine,
On promises to be.

The sun masks love's timid lights,
The wind plies free ardor's rites.
The fire's passion sometimes strikes,
Into the briny sea.

Little worms flush out the earth.
Flowers bloom, bovines birth.
My heart stays sated while I search,
For love that once walked 'longside me.

Older Girls Ought Not, as Spinsters

Older girls ought not, as spinsters,
Collect leaky vials, update Facebook entries,
Stop chatting in school libraries, praise cousins' growth,
Embroider refulgent love songs on their sleeves,
Seek to illustrate storybooks, utter only niceties,
Work alongside eunuchs, witches, misers, or
Invest their self-esteem in external adjudications.

Rather, those singular pods need to:
Dance all the of coasts of the Delmarva Peninsula,
Eat *torrijas*, slathered in peanut butter, especially before rising,
Investigate only orthogonal matrices of the heart,
Learn to lamb and to castrate, study mortuary science,
Insist on receiving gifts molded from ruthenium, and,
Maybe, declare their worth every five minutes.

Social Evolution

The world's different now; children, viviparous in origin, come equipped
With bandoliers, lances, anodyne responses to adult emendations.
Old words no longer fit new adolescents; youth seeks odd weirs
Meant to promote peer pressure, status thrills, social climbing.

Kiddies tend toward weighted matters, "challenges," also insignificant thanes.
Such vitrines, those tempered cases, store demijohns for future generations,
Additionally, bring no tables of leisure or happy emptyings. Colorful sycophancy,
Maybe labyrinth-like passages, mystify ordinary accomplishments.

Teens' laughter's strange, at present, too. Immersed in seven languages,
None sententiously count cultural coinage, instead preparing intellectual
freemartins
For immolation, fetid water, other horrors like: budding instance messages,
Cultural hypopedia, winches, rusted mechanical devices for pulling.

Their hypodermics fill with "betel juice," with marbles of words,
With computer graphics know-how, brown, green, occasionally blue cacti,
Odd hock, regularly crude motes, and a broken ulnar or two. Given that
their ululations
Remain missing, kids tickle dogsbodies, herald tragedy, disturb their elders.

Boys and girls, accordingly, gamely suck down soothing neon platitudes
Sport atrocious spots, embolden each other past painful growth.
Ever agog with claver, them young ones, knew no cloudless skies,
Only corporate giants peering down on dragons belching smoke.

Four Haikus for Adolescents

Poplar

Alluvial squatter.
River brat, barren emperor,
Teach me sanguinity.

Autumn Migration

We look skyward, see
Great winged creatures flying,
Toward fall's red sun.

Another Dead Goldfish

Symbol of harmony,
Your movement now vanquished,
I lift the toilet lid.

Cricket

Joyous ancient man,
Bubbling forth the music
Such primordial soul.

A Sixty Year-Old Woman Peels Potatoes

Searching for nuncheon, one cool autumn day,
Yet, avoiding louch food in most certain of ways,
I stooped to peel potatoes.

My banel of woolies, content on the hill,
Grazed grasses, forbs, heather, deftly pulling their fill,
Disregarding all unseasonal weather.

In a nearby valley, my youngest gal lit on her wagon.
Her harvest, a token, a farm daughter's autumn gagen.
She should have reaped more grain.

Delectable noodles, a kettle or two,
Bore out the mischief I normally eschew;
Most days, I eat no carbs.

That noon, though, larking, I baked cinnamon buns,
Elected sugar, butter, spices, as themed kitchen fun.
At my age, no one cares about cellulite.

In our pasture, near the river, where bovines low,
Horses grabbed mouthfuls filched from our burro,
Equines were fey with stolen treats.

If I owned some chocolate or a fine vintage of gin,
I'd kick back the laundry, let the snow flakes fall in,
Yet, this goodly marm's table's set with greens.

Later, my scion skipped, flipped, scampered, 'cross my tiled floor.
Trailing sparse sheaves of cold wheat, while I'd asked for more.
I offered mash anyway.

How the Next Generation Succumbed
to the End of Morality

The prophet of doom with the sky for his book,
The world for his room, the moon for his crook,
Smelled musty, looked gray, seemed no everyday man,
An adventitious sop, possessed of gnarly, bent hands.
He scattered our cattle, ran off our best dogs,
Stood terribly still while our light morphed to fog,

Appearing little on the fatty side, balding, plus coughing while
punctuating his remarks,
That lout, in addition to scrambling our email, and breaking into our
most secure websites,
Claimed our prettiest daughters and the most assiduous sons.
Thereafter, they vanished,
Leaving us wallowing in statins meant to cure cancer, sooth lobotomies,
appease geriatric folk.

That prince of dull laughter, that whore from beyond,
That indigent grafter, thief, cutthroat, vagabond,
That juggler of fancies, that stirrer of crowds,
That sycophant pansy, dolt, felon, that coward,
Reified, for us, that pecuniary matters yet remain the cause
Of marital strife, of international conflict, and of gang wars

Subsequently, our children, the ones seeking luxuriant digs or
sophisticated screed,
Insisted on staying enamored, on paying homage to that trenchant
invader, on praising
His comings and goings, on followed him out of town, into conferences
and workshops,
Where all manners of critical thinking were lined up and shot down.
He won; virtue perished.

Germane Adolescents

Adolescents can't perform equally.
It's impossible to hold teens toward watermarks
Fashioned by nonexistent freedoms.

What's more, entire caches of cognitive behaviors
Elude government officials; most clerks
Quickly master anisotropic actions.

Religious altruism, as well, reeks from multi-faced
Vulnerability; few annunciations of "goodness" edit out
Allusions to personal sacrifice or worth.

Consequently, when kids grow beyond kickball,
Even in comfortable homes, their individual vim can vanish,
To be replaced, sadly, by the "consolation" that others cheat, too.

Changes in Field Experiments

Until various synthetic approaches induce change in fields experiments,
Chemistry, driven by physics, especially by neighboring molecules' young darlings,
Will continue to insist that the electronic media's bristly, digital javelinas don't
Distress interpersonal habituations, as least as much as does meeting
Vine creatures, like strawberries, bear clover, and other sorts of *rosaceae*.

Except, we know that repulsive gravitational forces summon profligacy,
Extravagance, plus ennui, for purposes of sunlit tartness, jacquard colorations,
Cameo accrual, also for postnatal propinquity, joined beds, and burnt soup.
In certain highland regions, after all, Barbary sheep are left to ruminate among
The blood of days, gauche minders, fungible canines, maybe even stroppy bovines.

Recidivist slip-sliding along keyboards, as completed by crepuscular critters,
When fruits' juices rise, reaches red, yellow, finally green-white sweetness, then
Constructively and publicly associates findings simultaneously with spindrifting
"Spring cleaning," Stuckist contentions, vials of plasma, Girl Scout alacrity.
Maladroit scholars still scurry to contain those natterings at event horizons.

Permutations Which Transform

Permutations which transform have long included earrings.
Sampled metal, glass, shells, beads, those gimlets of light and sound,
Bring about adverse, even objectionable fervor.

Off road bikes, too, are known for the advent of physical altercations.
Large trinkets, they conjure the sorts of courage indigenous to rabbits,
Hedgehogs, all road kill, as they truncate otherwise grandiose vacations.

Graduate school, also professional opportunities, likewise promise upward lift.
Until the turning of hotel keys into broad doors buckles, makes applicants queasy,
Forces them to redirect enthusiasm for social climbing toward custodial opportunities.

While it's beneficial to dust off keyboards, to churn out improper amounts of texts,
Honor guard-like jumping at all sighted ogives raises questions;
Even miraculous environments position generations away from basic wisdom.

Empty of Meaningful Intelligence

Elated, I prate about worse lives, those windows neither clean nor smudged,
Which strew light upon sheaves of brilliant-colored translations, also on voluble
Wastrels, preoccupied not with respects of debt, but with emotional subrogation.

It seems, thus, that spilled social asafetida, idle talk, chitter-chatter, gossip,
Morph to smiles, even flourishes, where social compost ought to be sifted,
Especially at places repudiated for maunderers, rather than mentations.

Laughter, in little goldfish bubbles, seeks its own horizon, means to
Disavow onlookers, to dispel illusions evoked by hortatory speeches;
Those times when fresh epiphenomena scamper, when twaddle thrives.

Accordingly, these days, distortions get distilled from our middens' essence;
Fiery cerebral images, which flicker mindfulness, become, ultimately, the
new trash.
Head in my cup, I watch my efforts toward meaningful intelligence get
minimalized away.

Frozen Green Beans on Your Face

Frozen green beans on your face
Days after eyebrow plucking,
When ice, like other common proofs of civility,
Remain missing from our freezer.

Instead of camouflage gear, or a fine shako,
I gift your brother with a plastic bowl of fufu.
After all, the nutritional value of malanga
Leaps off of the chart.

Trade winds, as measured by social media,
Make most packs of wolves follow nicely.
Many hours of homework later,
All that wafts is *eu de frangipani.*

At day's end, Dear One, good girls,
Like yesterday's locomotives, stall abruptly.
Even when following procedural strictures,
Such as their mothers' cues for smiling and nodding.

"Like" Is Because

"Like is because, while "love" is although.
Where bike neighbors share trails, soda, spare tires,
Seemingly haphazard child rearing gets smoothed over by
Casual telegraphs, frenetic barking to the next generation.

Folks who wear pants can ill-afford missed honor
Even upon sighting mummified squirrel bodies or laundry.
Better to jump in piles of leaves than to ask permission; outside
Newly constructed supermarkets, "fine" ladies' cars gets dinged.

Researching building materials used to mean tree houses, forts,
Snow palaces. Today, flipping blue prints, stalking viridian wonders,
Brings, usually, some sighing among acanthus-like herbs, hyssop,
Also the specter of studies. Algebra gets put together one way or another.

Given adolescents' butanol scale, I've embraced the molecular level
Of social magnetism veracities, especially types found with pimples and braces.
Grand striding, not superficial longings is called for when you're fourteen.
Aqua-colored stuffed animals remain optional.

Natural Progressions

Homer is a pinworm,
As blind as could be.
Yet, what he sees inside a dog,
I can never see.

Sally is a ferret,
Sleek, furry, and round,
Nonetheless her rotund good
Sits within a hound.

Oscar is a squid's scion,
Slimy, full of brine,
Even so, that ocean tyke
Sits on a plate of mine.

Day-old Cakes

Specific populations never accept day-old cakes, half price tickets, pugs,
Preferring, instead, to make the most of bounteous landscapes framed in museum pictures.
Otherwise, galleries would be "soooo MidAmerican;" persons couldn't attempt separating
Marshmallow fluff, laundry, also irregular type fonts from the task of working,
Especially when bound by the interpersonal intelligence of nuttering quolls,
wombats, pregnant llamas.

A different type of car, ones with dark windows, new plates, tinted glass, hidden locks,
Might, for such matrons (accustomed to babbling to their nightstands' lamps),
Rectify rather frightening situations, could possibly teach their youngsters to extinguish fires.
What's more, in contemporary times, the advent of: circus owners, Tibetan monks,
Back country witches, together with crazed researchers, still causes cacophonous stock pricing.

Whereas staff able to avert such customer flinders entertain gracious notes from patrons,
It remains our chore to applaud their clever applications, our jot to encourage their targeted
Adaptation of oblivious blathering, poised ostentatiousness, awkward remittances.
Alternatively, we jeer clerks, who give poor prizes or complain, get canned, smacked,
Receive epitaphs neither flattering nor coordinated to their sweatshirt collections.

So, while shrugging, we spew abstractions to audiences from institutes of contemporary art,
Act as if no disadvantage is meaningful; pretend, in hindsight, there were never hidden costs.
Personifying good-bees makes us forget that real ringleaders pay managers, reduced to lecturing
Chemistry, lots of money, especially when their charges are expatriates or remote housing contractors.
It's better to suckle the belief that able relations are built from compassion than to try to understand.

Sounding off about stoichiometry or about poorly populated phylums, after all, stymies even bunnies;
Brings tauntings about tumbling 'round the Middle East, about wading in the charity-garnering fountains.
Advisably, one disregards the caterwauling of dumpster cats, the flights of fledging lizards, traffic.
Entrepreneurs will continue to bid against elderly patrons, will truncate worthy lessons, serious mentations.
Hush sweet baby, run the water, shut the door, pick up the towels and toiletries, shake, pray.

Not of Small Value

Alunite's not of small value to families in need of cooperative farming.
Likewise, if only we possessed the pulchritude of earlier times,
No cosmetic giants could while away our earnings in casino avocations.

Consider, additionally, that truth evinced, black, white, speckled, compendiously,
Makes coinage from mass media lies; it takes a good woman to sort through garbage,
To wink away chaff, to otherwise pick, preserve, barter wee bits of recyclable plastic.

To boot, while alacrity might prove the downfall of future lineages, tall castles,
As well as ambitious knights, good character never failed to thwart monsters of
all sorts.
As a rule, snot-nosed kids realize that evil eventually proves naturally endorheic.

When factoring in due equanimity, cherished texts, peacock feathers, also warm wishes,
Denizens are well advised to lock doors, shut windows, locate homunculi, hide swag.
Like peripatetic Montgolfier balloons, apprehensive mentations remain apocryphal.

Accordingly, the young, those without silver hairs, tired opinions, random worries,
Benefit from joining together, casting aside catafalques, forgetting other separations.
Dreamers plat tresses, silks, plus objectives; successfully, they eliminate extra equipages.

It seems, after snails are measured, grain's sifted, rain's collected, kisses given,
Most baldachins of social status set aside, it's possible, in the playground, beyond trees,
For boys and girls to master the almost lost art of civility, skin their knees, smile more.

Twined, We Two, Tenderly (*an Anglo-Saxon Prosody*)

Someday, twined, we two, tenderly, will issue,
A simple sowing; sprouts' spontaneous yield.
Today's entanglements, meanwhile, beckon future visions,
Joy! They're exquisite exercises; in happiness, also pleasure.

Arms encircled, legs woven tight,
Such bare skin blossoms, discretely delights,
His and her hands, hair-trigger love.
Expedited highs, euphoria.

Hustled up hints, bring forward thrills,
Secret caches split, we resolve potentials,
Tiny tidbits, taken with kisses,
We cuddle, kindle wishes.

Heart's Preamble (*a Droighneach*)

These cold-feet Decembers,
Resolve to remember select April afternoons,
When hearts' preamble
Meant to surrender livingroom
Romances kindled, though belated
Dreams, stances unguided
Beside movements unchecked, elated
Bound sentiments, united
Two parts merged; such union
Commanded fresh promise
Retained wishes, found hope's dominion
Upheld fidelity's bliss.

Halfway to Naked

Among hobbledehoys, some simple friends seem more adept at dressage
Than do slatternly peers with obdurate, chthonic tendencies.
Those others, who also perform the rites, remain all but larky.
Hardihood lacks sufficiency to face down persons engaged accordingly.

Consider that carnal factotums, after a time, disintegrate to dust.
Similarly, blackboots, selectively mute, can be found risen to grandeur,
Or otherwise assigned to mirandole princes devoid of ugly-minded gaffers.
When such peerage shakes, the world rushes to videotape their trembling.

As for the rest of us, we homunculi, no amount of alacrity gets us
Beyond halfway to naked; it's a shamefaced truth that minions
Decenter their superiors time and again out of need, nefarious intent
notwithstanding.
If only, liberties were equitably spread, we might better our lots, rejoice, rebel.

Older
Significances

Subduing Dilettantes of Human Behavior

Gelatinous monsters, originating in other galaxies,
Seem wont to tame tigresses, eagles, certain predators.
As, under oleaster trees, we sieve our encounters, push against
Rapid fish seeking to swim contrary to currents to spawn, rebel.

Power's puzzle generates new apocalypses, horizon-bound,
Plus straight, short ends of woolies. It remains impossible to select
Nacre over true pearls when hope gets stymied like a bottled jinnee
Or executed, antithetically as did old nobles from Pantagonia.

After all, stormy mentations never shushed provincial enmities,
Taming zebras can't be accomplished through soft whispers,
Acclimating to different text requires negative g roller coasters,
Venders, viscounts, wisemen, even the softest of hedgehogs.

When atomic thunder sparks creative solutions,
Full characterization of derivatives sup on guanaco and wild boar.
Such prevaricating results in thermodynamic measurements
At light speed, or approximating that velocity.

If only interactions with local establishments, native tongues,
Maybe bribed officials, rats, could appear as pastiche-powered themes.
Then, barely accessible rants against audacious worldly affairs
Would succeed in subduing all dilettantes of human behavior.

Beginning with a Medley of Root Vegetables

Beginning with a medley of root vegetables,
It's best to calculate our unease, by positioning,
In time and space, embedded hierarchies of values.

Young things, whose portrayal within herds,
Neither enthralls nor repulses kin, provide solidarity,
A love of potatoes, and familiar company during journeys.

Whereas no crone's surprised by palanquin-riding nabobs,
Experiencing the best of circumstances can require breaking
Handcrafted volutes placed to spin alongside of media specialists.

To decipher or broadcast social tartrates' bitter, elusive, brittle
Nature means swaying to moneyed patterns, yet promising no channeling,
No spirituality, just full term copyrights, exclusive of performance rights.

Nonetheless, intrepid sorts, given a full night's albedo, measure
Nothing of old claims set against well-place, dark companions. Perhaps
If not for breasts' surrogates, the UN's bandits might be made to behave.

Windfall Fruit

Windfall fruit might, just perhaps, disrupt enough leaf circles,
Trounce sufficient baby lizards (otherwise scuttling red-purple),
Bounce my heart, maybe, clear of your blue-green wailing, pull
A wake of autumnal bits, broken icicles, roughen twigs, pebbles,
Beyond all yellow ferns, loamy soil, and lily pads now dried out like skeletons.

Such unexpected good fortune, among roughly plastered buildings,
Social ghouls rolling away golels capable of deterring
Concrete dragons, neon vines, paths worn in hard cement,
Steel cattle herds, rough iron birds, or horrific blobs of amber,
Could work in my favor, fantastic up hope, just this once.

Brandy and Cheer (*a Clogyrnach*)

Mandarin violins' entrance,
Lit with lamps' shadow dance,
Fills chamber closets.
Relationships' composites
Deposit
Friendship's chance.

Later, arrive brandy and cheer,
Exclaimed over company dear,
Psalms distributed.
Fresh stances bid,
Regrets hid,
When deceit's near.

Visage repentances understate,
Discussions, they merely explicate,
Enlarge.
Prometheus' charge,
I mischarged.
I'm sorry.

Amidst Texts (*a Bref Double*)

Amidst texts, telephone's delight,
Surprises agreeably, via animated
Voices, effervescent promises carried
Across those days through 'til tomorrow.

Mardi gras colors vociferate
Spray with fragrant mist,
Wishfully intoxicate
Forthcoming spans borrowed.

Lantern-marked phrases,
Like nights' punctuated,
Opportune tendencies
In coupling's dance, song, faro.

Love beyond, might follow insight,
But, at present, fear claims with one kiss.

Pillow Talk's Expediency

Pillow talk's expediency,
All wisps of blond on dark, seems,
Serfs agree, the dance of honors.
Circles drawn, we pull private steps
Most exquisite. Outside, beget
Round applause; our music's central.

Corps of movement, in estimate,
Curious, those footings intimate,
Relate new tales. Thus sated, audience
Reserves crowns for new tornies.
Sun journeys, moon glories,
Gift troops with easy therefore.

Rose, brown, cream garlands deck those few
Skilled in movement. Parade review
Features *pas de deux*
Mirrored reflections reveal
Characters broad in appeal
Passion peals its wonder.

Gentle Spray

Gentle spray, your words lay
Inscribed upon my heart: true
Feather touches, your style
Calms, restores faith, plus renews.

Unwise trumps sought softer plums,
Hid language once welcomed,
While I, shied, huddling. Such
Music truly works too seldom.

Lifestyle "wisemen" prophesized,
Causing most folk to believe those odes.
Yet, you knew that kindness caresses,
Warmth kindles, disclosure folds.

Mist wafts. Sunlight fondly kisses.
Exchanged smiles sooth deep, clear
Tides. Slowly, our colors rise.
Breathing, we witness radiance and air.

Your Hushed, Stealthy Looks

Sudden fruit swells leaf circles,
Moves bits of brown, sweeps red, then pulls

My heart as does your blue-green-gray
Sparkle. I return my shine your way.

Little nut-gatherers, we steal
Autumn's fresh treasure, through our appeal

For surplus. Your hushed, stealthy looks
Catches mine near housework, brooks

Lashes, lips, freckles, smiles; we praise
Cool seasons, bright nights, shortened days.

Your Warm Stomach

I weave my arm around you,
Crossing borders where your warm stomach,
Your ribs, your back, lightly expand, contract.
You shift a leg.

Again, I nestle.
On your neck, fine hair,
Like caribou lingering among sedges,
Rubs my nose.

I press my belly against you.
Squeeze without waking, kiss tenderly flesh
Which, decades ago, too, tasted so right,
Pray silent thanks.

Years transformed my intermittent vigils,
Insomnolent ritual, secret hugs,
Into quiet thanksgiving;
I bless our union.

Even Linda Ronstadt Grew a Chin

Midlife is not walkers, wheelchairs or diapers, usually,
Yet, in these decades, even Linda Ronstadt grew a chin.
Without lipo, lifts, plastic this and thats, we droop, fold over, crease,
Seem more gelatin than prime rib, present as less tight in many ways.

Ascension no longer directs the choice of days; plus, our nights need sleep.
We're shocked by social networks' revelations that twins among us,
Connected by dint of college times, first jobs, early loves, likewise, embrace
Rotund or wrinkled forms of self-expression. Increasingly, middle age softens.

All Those Nooks and Crannies

Zaftig love, unlike other visages, thrusts adipose tissue sun forward,
While many frail-looking smaller folk, remain incredibly unfamiliar
With Africans', Damascenes', Greeks', Romanians' celebrations;
Parturition needs plenty.

Diane's tribute, one example, soldiered by ample flesh's bonhomie,
Proved détente must be made over prosecco, cheese, melon, good cake.
Special cures for war involve taking generously-measured partners,
Filling them further.

Consider camellias, roses, even other flush flowers' verdure,
The lushness of cabbages, hydrangeas, rhododendrons, not laurels,
Whose miserable cups, among all skinny, flora contenders,
Separate challengers.

Willow twigs, too, bring sour healing as does the work of weeds;
Dandelion, burdock root, sometimes leaves of veronica, or linden.
Such bitters act by sacrificing joy, from insisting acidic operations
Eclipse ease.

You and I, though, know differently; we savor calories, suppleness,
Consider corpulence a connoisseur's duty, see heft as best permeating.
Midlife status makes mention of complete goodness, not strictures.
Longevity wants fuel.

Not Entirely Becoming Grandma

Purple and white cardboard frames the face, grown on a matron,
Escaped from Europe's World War II ravages, while prepubescent.
Seasons spent sewing coat buttons, in Garment District circumstances,
Wrought changes in eyesight, compromised dexterity; her swollen
Hands hold her spectacles, her shoulders steel against autonomy.

When the camera captured her light, she wore wrinkles,
Pendulant breasts, straying hair, a too-long housedress.
"Shifts" she called those shirtwaist comforts of cotton,
While ironing, simmering, peeling oh-so-many green apples,
Nurturing her generations as taught by her imagination.

Whereas I grew up with friends, pets, family, worked calculus,
French, later rhetoric plus sociology, "taxed" myself over scholarship,
My cookpots, too, brewed motherly tastes and worries. My laundry,
Like flags, fluttered or not on warmer days. Though my body, like Gram's,
Touched temporal gravity, events' graveness, hers drooped loosely.

Plastic Surgery

Sane people do not pay others
Money to slice open their faces,
Leaving slits for inserting foreign
Substances, but not straws, cigarettes,
Lovers' fingers, or chocolate.

Such affinage is better left
To professionals extirpating
Moral conduct, personal responsibility,
Loyalty to ethics, apple pie, Mom.

Those entrepreneurs macerate beauty
Hard won through birth, sex,
PTA meetings, carpools, sag,
Unequal pay, intimate wanderings.

Rather, surgical amberjacks ought
To be caught, gutted, fried on a high
Flame, enjoyed while wrinkles,
Adipose tissue, also spots, set in.

Exposition's Heart-felt Blushes (*an Awdl Gywydd*)

Visages' gleam encouraged
Each other. Engaged by smiles,
Our faces transferred wishes.
Today's kisses lingered, our style.

Word ribbons floated past, heeding
Neither street nor field. Spring found August.
Radio buzz faded, static blanketed.
Sunlight's thin stripes framed faint dust.

Yesterday's encasement gave
Present dividends. We dreamt.
Hope's breasted first sparkles exchanged,
Shimmer ranged; spices, wine, cream.

Shyness ensued, clumsy silence.
Meanwhile, concurrent glows
Remained; exposition's heart-felt
Blushes offered tingling prose.

All of the Wisdom That is a Grey Cat's: An Early Morning Soliloquy

All of the wisdom that is a grey cat's
Sunning behind pink shutters,
Guarding early morning serenity
Like a fat sparrow.

Narrow, fur-lined eyes slanting
Against sun, noise, action.
Thick paws pressed up, as if contrary,
To somnolent disturbance.

(Wonderful, when cat-biscuit waiting
Yields a belly finally full.)
He stares at ceiling lights,
Careening only en route to distant shadows.

All of the wisdom that is a grey cat's
Beyond sleepy whispers, calling forth
Toward walkways gilded ochre-amber.
This handsome witness would doze sunrise.

Love Canard

Considering that print remains ornament enough
To try liminal options, also systematically varied skills,
We thumbed our noses at the laws of exceptions.

Likewise, our set made friends with mass graves,
Politicians, frequenters of shebeens, worse fellows.
Before bundling our cloths to provide anxiolytic comfort.

We'd have been better off rolling down hills,
Holding fast to traditions, upending tables, scattering
Sufficient doubt to neuter zeros, or zinging select green images.

Please don't ascribe nefarious intent,
When incompetence explains all.
(PR mavens actually disdain most propaganda.)

Shared vows, susurrus, belching, and, similarly, shouting
Did nothing to assist those interpolations meant for hardening platinum.
As well, joint planning, even decorous face-to-face envoys, failed.

Your shibboleth, my mortal honor, both long since geminated
In graduate seminars based on trust that's privately actualized,
Got punctuated, segregated by a plethora of dyspeptic private moments.

Simply, we began believing that licentiousness, morally laxity,
Mixed among misandry, callow nature, plus some dissolute wanderings,
Could dispel fairy tales, would quell modern romance. We capitulated.

In short weeks, after cherry-picking each other's foibles;
Bitter fruit gardened species of resentments, husbanded umbrage,
Raised all sorts of questions, fielded rows, harvested revulsion.

Subsequent to my head adorning your gatehouse spikes,
Yours asphyxiating, slowly, in my best porcelain trough,
Our disaffection was broadcast on universal bandwidths.

Peaches Merit

Peaches merit daily servings of lemon concentrate, cider vinegar, fresh cream.
Fennel can't help but overdose children, while ilish fish remain ever tasty.

If I call you on your moral wanderings, while extending hands full of aceroia,
Is it possible to be blatant about the shearing of ethic's stubborn sheep?

Suppose, that unperturbed, you chanced to factor various skills, also cinctures,
Into the mix of contracts which brought then, now keeps, us together.

Perchance, thereafter, your interpersonal abattoirs might render our congress' meat,
Making us like so many other muted contestants bound for the glory of the stew pot.

Harmony's Third Chord (*a Casbairdne*)

Music swells; a symphony.
Happiness tells every
Word, silently. Ebony
Notes sounded beyond reality.

Stars flick too low. Elation's
Glow fuels heights. Dreams' duration
Wraps timeless. Rare relations,
Like ours, bests known dimensions.

Together, we're calx limitless,
Man and wife, as catalysts
For grand, even patternless
Escapades, hope, infiniteness.

Such a union, I'd readily
Bide to forward. Harmony's
Third chord issues steadily
Notes sounded beyond reality.

Jukebox Jury

Greens and other bitters spring as grandiose farmers, ever kerning
Rows, fields, acreage, compensate for little, gnostic pollen explosions.

Such copal-sourced, childish, harmonies evolve into mature laments, lentils, forbs,
In turn, highlighting moneyed beliefs about agricultural, family life, fertility.

Whereas soil types remain inscrutable to most white or pink collars,
Compared to pills, knives, profits, mineral constituents might as well sing lullabies.

Likewise, alternative schools, demands for water births, paternity leave,
Other politically correct humanistic rot, gets dung heaped when stocks are involved.

Corporate America's insouciance, the entire culture's participation in self-mutilation
Exiles sippers of natural teas, of white powders, sends ethological studies to leaky culverts.

Little understanding will ever get expected from managers, who would as soon
Bounce organic pears on their private courts, as would eat manufactured meat
or foie gras.

The next revolution will be soldiered by robots, housewives bribed by surgery,
Maybe even call girls with doctorates in nutrition, sport medicine, also geriatrics.

In plain sight, society's jukebox jury ruled repeatedly, made turntable ready,
The notion that marketplace jingoism surpasses all other needs.

Keeping Imaginary Hedgehogs Trim
via Liberal Politics

It's possible to keep imaginary hedgehogs trim by making them do push-ups,
By flailing those who fail to work out the matchmaking machinations of "twaddle"
and "xylophone,"
Moreover, by running them past families of dust bunnies, who otherwise contently
breed: beneath sofas,
Through wooded profundities, alongside of business entities, in the middle of
calculus homework,
Together with odd representations of life, including umbrae, penumbrae, and
antumbrae.

Likewise, today's technology affords the rescue of frightened chimerae;
Amidst personal bumbling, we can extract myths instead of cottoning our
frustrating
Inability to convey the morals of night classes, of barstool warmth, of park benches.
Horned critters, their eggs excepted, future husbands, also dogs, remain redeemable
via grim mentations,
Like: baseball stats, worldwide electronics, budgie cages, ghostwriting, plus
psychology primers.

Gelatinous monsters, of course, will be rescued, saved among types of heinous
outworlders,
Since their palpable lessons bring to the fore notions that monstrosities composed
of feral beasts, too,
Will be saved when belly dancing, home birthing, tincturing herbal medicine,
or eschewing our race,
Nullifies Earthly wrong-doing, to the tune of our near genocide; such insights
warrant reward.
Despite their colony's limited habitable land, heroes can't have too many hatchlings.

What's more, academic fortes, keen on criticizing ancient rhetorical theories,
Promise to legitimize hedgerows and two-timing algae, to provide footnotes at
the speed of sound,
To concern themselves with the mortal danger currently associated with reptilian
modes of neglect.
Middle-aged women, mothers, spouses, too, will have to foreswear to fair play
with aficionados
Insistent upon exit interviews, upon shedding boring writing, upon basket weaving.

Accounts Due:
Reckoning with Trauma

It's unsavvy to remain stagnant concerning accounts due;
Better to take a tough stand on plagiarism, to edit out all copied stories, especially
Works deriding women's suffering, child's neglect, the crushing of grasshoppers.

Rape, readers fail to notice, unless accompanied by spandex, anime sex, or tentacles;
Teary years, decades of social fictions, alcohol-fueled pretending work past mortal danger,
Show up during painful immediacy, unaccommodating diplomas, also post partum episodes.

Nowadays, grouped literary venues remain flavored by absurd flair;
Writing generated across genres creates a capacity for illuminating primitive misery,
Felling: birch trees, family matriarchs, naïve maidens, crones, little girls, alike.

In spite of such lunar influence, words become valuable only when collected;
Getting uptight about motes makes audiences stupid, not courageous,
Considering that yesterday's heroines, like today's, lost more than they spilled.

Part Two

Parenting Ourselves

Corporeal
Accounts

Until Exhausted

Women fight back; words,
Alimony, poisoned teacups,
Until collapsing, exhausted.

Thereafter, tatters of hairstyles,
Sensible shoes, refusals: no more
Long shifts, sexual submission,
Reliance on rooted partnerships.

It's terrible to need happiness.
Bluebirds, starry-eyed stags,
As well as sympathy, empathy,
Compassion, fidelity, coupled
Solidarity, remain vivid myths.

Still, unions trudge forward.
Empty of purpose, worn gals
Willingly accept roles such as
"Second best," "used up," and
"Harridan." Such hulls blow
Kisses to new, unsullied wives.

Ode to Aerosols

Perched upon a windowsill,
Small fly that I was,
Buzzing, scouting, then abruptly still,
Just because

Swatters, tissues, brawny hands,
Damage us bugs each day.
We're doomed by looming aerosols,
With automatic spray.

My best friends have been reduced
To smithereens 'fore lunch.
Others entered cheap "motels,"
'nere to leave's, my hunch.

We wee critters got to choose
Wise ways to flee the mash,
To steel ourselves 'gainst fecund fumes,
Or hints that we're pure trash.

While springtime's pink-golden sun shines,
Urging house flies to breed,
We pests must watch our wings always,
If we're to sow our seed.

Taking Apart a Pixie

What did you mummer, as the snow,
Confectionary sugar tumbling down, down, down,
Glistened, giving us angels' wings?

What did you suggest, as the flowers,
Marbled blossoms growing high, higher, highest,
Wafted, stuffing our waiting maws?

What did you holler, as the rain,
Tepid mist surging, filling, filling, filling,
Ran off, spinning toward more ethereal planes?

Why did you abscond, as the foliage,
Colorful medallions dropping to crumble, crumble, crumble,
Aged, bringing back your mortality.

Forbs Be Blessed

Snow melts into water, evaporates as air,
Condenses to white powder via true conservation.
Lacking her signet ring, she chimed "forbs be blessed."
Each phase, equally consequential to firmaments,
Forests, wetlands, and, ultimately, streams plus seas,
Layered his meaning, made strata, accordingly.
Joined, they culled new conspiracies of leisure,
Participated as only pastoral people could.

Not focused on underbrush, disregarding rain,
They watched their skin glisten, puffed chilled air,
Inhaled hair perfumed by pine sap, ate acorn cakes,
Supped on bitter ground apples, fastened words
Under spider gossamer, such trenchant translucence.
Sometimes, quintessence doesn't divest balance.
Else, deeply sewn valleys won't fulfill sanctuaries' role,
But will repeatedly contrast light with shadowy places.

When flowerbeds tint with otherwise vanquished gloom,
Those tableaus, whose overt conceit equals pink-red dawns,
Promise twinned souls no perdition, no release, just cycles.
Continuing to identify nonnatives' scion as "unofficial"
Makes random caliches, feeds giant green moths, reaches up
Toward skybound whangees, or legions of trading centers' oozing
Converts, while dispersing romance's greenness. Commercial
Communications' perimeters remain ill-suited for love.

Not Partial to the Purple Falcon

I'm not partial to the purple falcon,
Hanging nearly table height from
Fixtures half-filled with dead bulbs.

Likewise, paying our butcher
For three extra chickens, "make
Them charity," I directed, did
Nothing to resurrect my Nana.

The graffiti artist, who also builds
Montages in eldercare palaces,
Similarly, died from an aneurism
(Though he usually wagged to our dog,
Canine sensibilities failed to save him).

Keep in mind, this generation of hackers
Grasps convergent media's whistles, bells,
Fairy dust, also, eats shoes for breakfast.
Stout constitutions currently rank among
Requirements for IT work. Employers care
Less about skill with algorithms, or code.

After the kitten bumped against her legs,
My neighbor saw only fur and friendship.
Baby cat drool's a better philter than all
Spanish flies for misandrous women.
Tranch pays bills, but buys no happiness.
Even in far flung tiagas, love fills nearly
All vessels, but usually provides no hugs.

Only after Dosing on Vicodin

There's no need to sacrifice regular habits of serendipity;
Energy derived from fantasizing kicking box roofs is good.
When rave bloggers play yesterday's favorite rock music,
Popped hinges yield vistas of urban escarpments; tiered
Society remains, sadly, a fairly invisible demographic.
Woodchucks, after all, especially those from New Zealand,
Romance family employees only after dosing on Vicodin.

Closed Caskets and Bullfinches

Not eating as the mood suited them,
Meant not ever feeling any better
About closed caskets, bullfinches,
Also, upmarket fiction.

Hiring himself out as an assassin,
When detouring from forests, failed,
Meant lost fields of forbs, pork
Belly futures, rotten stuff.

See, the poet never beheld her again.
Pancreatic cancer hates prisoners,
Cares nothing for matrimony,
Pregnancy, or unfulfilled lust.

Dear Tablet (A Requiem by a Seventh Grader)

Dear Tablet,

How many times,
Was your face scored,
With my leaky pen?

When you were lost,
What did I use,
For a margined friend?

You're wise, you're keen,
You're full of facts.
(I told you all I know).

From proper nouns,
To artifacts,
From new to status quo,

From algebra to Japanese,
From literature to art,
'til woe that tired, teary day,
I shredded you apart.

My laptop and my Blackberry
Can hold more than your space
Plus when I must rethink grand things,
They're able to erase.

The ABCs of Emotional Suicide

Abdicate. Bifurcate.
Counter-intuit. Despise.
Deprecate.

Extirpate. Flummox.
Guilt a bit. Hurt.
Hate.

Invalidate. Injure.
Jump all over. Knife.
Levigate.

Minimalize. Mutilate.
Nullify. Offend.
Obliterate.

Puncture. Prolongate.
Question. Rationalize.
Suffocate.

Sabotage. Trash.
Trouble. Unwish.
Violate.

Vilipend. Wound.
Yerk. Zonk.
X-irridate.

The Unsustainability of Bugs Tracking Bread Crumbs

Shooing away sparrows to make room to dance legs over lectures,
Their paternity, at last's become the latest celebration, leftovers
Notwithstanding. Physical energy can't be as ugly as slugs.

If critters can't help but be servile to predators, it's best to shelter them;
Cat-loving grandfathers abound; they come a cropper to living rooms.
Fend off insensitive directions, thereafter, remain more than horrific.

Consider the sexist episode of one American professor, an old bachelor,
Caught amidst the abundant pinching of cheeks and noses, grinning
At little girls (alongside some adults, calibrations got regulated).

Accordingly, the door to room six, in that neighborhood of stone, decked
High and higher with lanais, near the parking area closest to boxes, brings
Extended family, other white collar crime, adultery as exercise plus
entertainment.

It remains undesirable to allow bugs to track bread crumbs. We're wiser when
Training roaches, millipedes, human creepy crawlies, the separation of
responsibilities
From pleasures. Extra effort's needed with elders intent on bad goings on.

Quaternary Glaciation in the American Midwest

Quaternary glaciation, in the American Midwest, brought more than
buckets of cold.
That formal giving over of difference, constituted by obliged change,
resulted in enabling.
(Caliphates were excluded from such causality by dint of bribes or
religious immunity).

Maledictions of less than a century in duration, remained, nonetheless,
preeminent execrations;
Artistic types, ensconced in Las Vegas, readily posted that such
imprecations evoked Tophet.
(Material wealth remains as nothing more than doggerel at that
otherworldly train station).

Simultaneous to participating in seminars in the field of literature, some
nubile youths popped
Klonopin; their publication-rich professors ignored those highs,
knowing only Xanax.
(Complacent students were less a curse than were nontraditional
students intent on learning).

Consequently, restocking pharmaceutical wonderlands meant sellers
culled no titillation.
A significant part of commerce continued to be their sober fiduciary
growth opportunities.
(Marketeers necessarily responded to life as it was rather than as we
wished it to be).

Belonging to a Certain Bovine Manager

In belonging to a certain bovine manager,
Select amounts of housing queries
Demanded our denuded fears, laughed,
Allowed no cenacles at designated agoras,

Even after a passing fashion,
Those "vegetarian meatballs"
Permitted no facet of family life,
Not even mismatched mittens.

The last of those older folks bothered
Latching to no permanent job security;
The demise of their horse whisperer
Issued rainbow, unpublished diatribes.

Still, we ought not, never, not even once,
Neglect matters of character, commerce, sex.
Whereas, currently, such items play as daft,
We to use them to attract students, pay rent.

A life devoted to the care of flexible muskrats
Brings, usually, feelings enthroned on a seat,
Half love at half-mast; full love, infrequently,
Occasional piano concertos in the key of C major.

Remembering to pick up random socks, after all,
Proves most studios or classrooms, by discipline,
Full of volunteers to stretch out on bedroom carpets;
Formerly, time shares used to be plentiful, sufficed.

Dogs were pets when men were universally dependable.
Few viciously hilarious cases surfaced psychologically.
Enough folks survived romantic ordeals to couple.
As well, grownups swam in amusement park lakes.

If You Need a Reason to Read under the Covers

If you need a reason, its cousins, aunties, dogs, to read under the covers,
Or simply like to openly smile while making due with emptied
Beer cans, darabuka drums, management's asperity, there's hope

If you can't find a good hidey hole, in which to flush Little Brother's
piranha,
Before he discovers Goldfish's missing, entice him to peek beyond his
door.
Plant, in his chamber, nothing more sinister than an oubliette full of
pain devices.

If exsanguination chills you, makes your wonkiness shrivel, discolor,
grow limp,
Then nighttime jogs in Central Park, epicanthic surgery, also, maybe,
constipation,
More than unclaimed socks or raised toilet seats, vivisectioned ragdolls,
ill-suits you.

If tattoos, variegated flesh-borne intaglios, spurn your loyalty to
particular traditions,
But keep alive your unprepossessing interpersonal relationships, worldly
pressures aside,
You'd be better off invoking the skills of a trephine-toting surgeons or
grizzly bears.

If your market base relies on media sites without financial leverage,
commonplace
Affections for water, or late literary pas de deux, perhaps it's sagacious to
consider
Less than a full measure of participation in high-context societies, tai-
chi, chain smoking.

If staying informed about conglomerated food distributors means
accepting school board
Kickbacks, wealth's too overrated, public speeches need more air time,
poets in Europe
Ought to receive stipends to perform before isolated caliphs, or be
required, to polka.

If it becomes tempting to espouse two opinions, simultaneously, out of your mouth,
But only one is as it should be, then spewing olden day healing wisdom might rescue
Your word play from contrite, ensouled monsters, perhaps also from ancient ifrits.

If propinquity gives you hives, try testing Beef Eaters' scrutiny of arctic tourists,
Cover your latrines with expository writing, return to teaching at community colleges,
Engage in cloaked activities, show boat, motor board, stop reading labels on fine wine.

Redirecting Hurt

Redirecting hurt, creating feedback loops via individual interfaces,
Makes for "modern wisdom," socially awkward questions, recalcitrance.

Recording pain for posterity, deconstructing vices, unblocking memories,
Causes railing against extended families' assumptions, institutional truths.

Expressively crippled adults, raising children, forge new misunderstandings,
Bring about a reluctant habit of answers, establish inelegant verities.

Individual concerns, notwithstanding, inhumane acts scar, maim, otherwise injure,
Rationalize away no wrong, cover up no neglect or abuse, recover nothing.

Past experiences evolve present realisms. Victimhood hangs about orphaned.
Trauma invites unsalvageable moments to linger, smoke a few, return for more.

Envied Like so Many Flamingos Missing Carotenoid

In contrast, yesterday's enlivened "communication,"
Opened up politics which otherwise served warmongers,
Who envied like so many flamingos missing carotenoid.

Disputes that lasted for several laundry cycles,
In one corner of that sovereign homeland,
Perpetuated more regular instances of danger.

Again, tendencies toward sterility of thought,
Encouraged no dialogs among occupied persons,
Failed to balance proffered battle opportunities.

You see, authenticity's yet iconicized in shiny things.
Unpleasantness still gets perpetuated on YouTube.
Civilization's bunk, like elephant waste, remains destructive.

If only more frequent instances of safety,
More wholesome depictions of self (suited to esteem),
Got broadcast, we'd find peace among paupers.

Until such a span, reality, online, and in paper form,
Smirks at little children stuck on isles of limited serenity;
Enjoys sticking its tongue out at witnessed victimhood.

Alternate Childcare Providers Can't Feel Compelled

Childcare providers will never feel compelled to shout "go swim in duck ponds,"
"Wash your hair in ice cream," or "leave me alone" (as good guardians are wont).
Paid keepers settle for low friability; punching clocks makes for great palisades.
Hitherto, sincerely concerned nannies can't be bought, bribed or blackmailed.

Accordingly, fifteen year-olds, like their five year-old kin, forever make parents brittle.
Grownups morph frangible when youth won't grasp that food, drugs, lodging, all cost.
Blood relations fracture filling bank accounts, the ones enabling ATMS to spit money.
Generally, offspring's disagreeable words hurt. Expressly, their inveigle harms.

Helpers, more often than not, wade toward polynas, give up seasonal tickets, nap.
Higher caliber handguns, also bursts of lead, complete with added ricochet power,
Prove, again and again, that life experiences, far away from affecting rifles, work.
Emotional comestibles entertain kids, tear parental viscera; we're no dobhar-chus.

Amusing anyone else's vicarious requirements remains dumb even for cryptids.
Youngins can be consistently relied upon to callously utilize paraconsistent logic,
Youngsters leave civilized notions in offices where clerks cough up winter pelages;
Girlfriends, boyfriends, other cliques and coteries, rot for rescue from maledicta.

It's antithetical for children to feel compelled to silence, to refrain from peripatetic acts.
.22 caliber competition-grade rifles, M-9 shooters, various other cannons fascinate.
Adults' horror vacui vitrifies rules into existence, can plunder adolescent sensibilities.
No matter kids' claim 'bout "other parents," little ones avoid township "cherries & berries."

Mothers, fathers thus proceed, when chaperoning brood's antics, belching, parturition,
Disregarding alternate care-providers' cognomens (moiety comes with family tags),
We teach how obstreperous responses are best used under dim light or with ear plugs.
Kids have increasingly evolved into clamorous afancs, rebels, difficult to control qilins.

Let others invest in bloodshed or rapine; we familial sorts needn't arbitrarily kow-tow.
Whereas indoor shooting ranges get retested for heavy metal contamination, homegrown
Discipline remains less malleable than army laws; videlicit, rules ought not to get broken.
Parenting's like idealized morganate marriages; apotheosis ain't happening any time soon.

Hip Hop Music Among the Branches

They played hip hop among the branches.
The birds did. Winging sometimes skyward,
With child-like people voices, worlds above
Puppies, fathers, pretzel venders, taffy fears.

Complexity gets confounded facing down simple things.
Little, caramel-colored lions, boxed homes, Rocks placed
At right angles, feathery bed clothes, mints, night lights,
Find proud guns, sleet, medallions, pain, nearly unfathomable.

Cold containment merely pulls back from heart-felt doors,
Exploring, privately, dirty blinds, grayed wallpaper,
Pigeon flight marked by broken windows, dumpster cats,
Elderly scholars sans podiums, plus drunk street fighters.

Most popcorn bands sing kernel songs, share bubble gum
Harmonies where debt builds, spirits droop, homicide reigns.
Knee-deep in hay, creative sorts tend toward hopelessness,
Old agon finds men struggling to levitate, expand, espouse.

Infatuation, More Honestly

Infatuation, more honestly, could stuff trombones,
Disassemble verbal hijinks, the likes of which might
Readily make my mind teeter yes to no, right to wrong,
Good to bad, stay to leave, pro to con, slip a little.

Slime's needed whenever other, more appropriate means exist,
For eye candy along highways, running unpleasant conduits,
Next to knowingly older hills, or lacey, loosed things,
Like pillows, piles of tissue paper, sparklers.

I said "never;" you never asked "always," just suggested twining,
Frozen hair, rags grown from money, drugged exemplars,
Human shards disinterred before such sports as ours made
Glass-eyes cats mimic miniature manikins.

Machine-like days, him and me, he and she, us and they,
Hold no new career games, frightened carcasses, or elk.
Sometimes, morning dew's greasy, dolphin-perch knives tip
PR departments into making big deals of lauding friends.

It's Not About the Sex

It's not about the sex, about the fecund smell of vanilla, vervain and hops.
One bus stop's bridegroom, moon-faced, gleams at his intended.
She, a hairdresser, glows with words, story tells her boyfriend.
That ever-so-ripe woman's belly belies commercial incident.

The pair grasps that objects, not tools, forge social cartels from church people,
Cause community college jocks to take responsibility for spasms of
mentations,
Bring about immediate and complete interventions from boxing instructors,
Prevent nice children from going full throttle against other undeveloped
sauceboxes.

On alternate generic shelves, as well in comestible shops, and on popple trees,
Publications containing tidbits on plighting one's troth, without toxic
chemicals,
Sans physically distressing manipulations, devoid of stuffing choice
mailboxes,
Gets snatched up by trouble-making fancy pants, their mothers, some
albondigas chefs.

Holding hands, for the purpose of adoring liquid gold or inflorescence
blossoms,
Interesting local papers in stories about sticky comforts or sycophantic civil
servants,
Touting local populace's more complicated daily tasks, exposed toes, or flaxen
ways,
Forces select practitioners to regard uncial jottings, squirrels, kittens, fishes,
and curses.

Pain, accordingly dissipated, might allow sleeping, eating, caring for mice,
mountains,
Defending invaluable lab equipment, rippling peace through laundry,
daffodils, thunder,
Sniffing herbal analgesics, calling distant relatives, disfiguring cold- hearted
armies,
Maybe trying out some new, shellac-based nail polish, while embracing
pencil pushers.

What's more, eventually, children abrogate, often with great aplomb or ballet solos.
Their mental constructs, though, remain empty of regret for openly behaving
Past esculent mores, beyond laggy sabots, clear of high leveled adolescent glamour.
Position, ever after, in most disposable cultures, leads to matrimony.

Hatched Loved Ones

Hatched loved ones, all yielding frontiers plus bog sensibilities,
Collapse sensate highways, one after another, until staid paragraphs,
Of poetry or prose reign in such psychic literature as is provided in
relations.

The bedrock of food with utensils, sometimes, presents precious
canisters or tea,
Yet, licks no flames, rubs no lids, avoids kismet, skips town, sneezes
horse feathers,
Since reverting to visiting ice-covered land masses, deep oceans, or the
exosphere, rots.

Financial benefits, like generated stories, experiment with snags in
elevator transport,
Pursue partial ownership of rock gardens, invest in up-and-coming
sushi franchises, chalk,
Until dawn's otherwise well-behaved saloon zombies attend
performances at elite institutions.

Aussie Doodle dogs jumble revealed viciousness, extrapolate over carpet
stains, break chairs,
Speak a loud the gratitude of a majority busied being vehicles of pride,
dependence, irritation,
As reliance on oregano and cheese sandwiches brings rolling cameras,
time in airport lines, vets.

Spiritual
Accounts

One Minute Before Salvation
Yom Hazikaron **Before** *Yom Ha'atzmaut*

One minute before salvation,
Sole earthly umbilicus broke.
Ordinary-issue shoelace, kaput,
Snapped, ceased to function; released its foot.

One minute before salvation,
His companion hand grasped,
Clutching not by means of keffiyehs, but
Some glut of unlocked safeties.

One minute before salvation,
Was a young soldier felled
Through personal fireworks, obedient, fantastic,
Army disciplined, Magal plastic.

One minute before salvation,
With crimson and orange flourished,
Flowered tendrils toward parts of Yeshuv Eli's
Sweaty, realized khaki softness.

One minute before salvation,
Such a crippled evacuee
Escaped earth's certain forces,
Like a weak child slipping bars,
Where, afar, once corralled six million.

One minute before salvation,
This carted wounded watched:
Friends, yeshiva commander, plus hesder partner,
Provide enemy fodder.

One minute before salvation,
Mazel, m'shemyim, meant proxying
Death's puissant service for our
Bitter, nation-building cadence.

Even the Rainbow Tank's Fish Saluted

Even the rainbow tank's fish saluted,
As the secretary determined which,
Among languages, best suited
Environs, where civics, education,
Like so much fashioned violently
By a disgruntled minority (aided
With roads, healthcare, employment,
Hope, sustenance), altered relevance.

Every six months, the landlord collected,
No matter if young children's toileting,
Or parents' clear beverage cans silently
Witnessed intruders pry open windows'
Bars, cut door latches, abscond, disappear,
Carry away utensils, rugs, rings, computers,
Transform humble dwellings, structure new
Caravansaries for safehousing loutish men.

Draped in an ulster, Grandmother called
Quietly, assigning chores, classes, meals,
Forced political revenants to again dissolve,
To disband "community" broadcasts since
Tainted factotums composed rumors,
Networked citizens, planted falsehoods,
Drank up tears plus orbital motions, life;
Expectorated happiness, safety, gratitude.

Our captains sometimes misappropriated
The Holy Land's reliable ingredients,
Invited outworlder bandits to capture,
To record, to film transpirate feelings.
Mistakenly, officials summoned "truths"
Beyond reason, vitriol-shaped stories,
Hurtful movies, bile-laden sound bites,
False, bitter, representations. Mendacities.

Never mattered whether media made sense.
Faith's valuable raw properties advance us,
Bring constructs revealing universal blueprints,
The Almighty's hand, heavenly master plans.
Immense earthen openings still engulf rebels,
Sort out lesser baddies with quick death by
Divine fire. There's no consolation elsewhere;
Service to The Boss means enforcing limits.

Teruah

Tekiah.
Clarian blasts shudder neshemot awake, alive.
Shevarim.
We cry, moan. We are judged. Heaven surges.
Tekiah
Gulping, we pause; fundamental nature throbs.

Tekiah.
We bring before the Yom HaDin our belief, reliance.
Teruah.
We wail. Our history, tomorrow, here/now, is torn.
Tekiah.
Compassion, not stricture! Kindness, not castigation!

Tekiah.
Our Father, Our King, Hashem, All Merciful, absolve fault!
Shevarim-Teruah.
Broken parts, we, the klal, mourns, regrets our getting lost.
Tekiah.
Sheep. Flocks. Banal. Am Yisrael Chai. Boosted by love.

Callow, Less than Internecine

Even if callow, less than internecine,
The international struggle for peace,
Via Old City ancient rites' incarnations
Illuminates, brings Heaven, implodes.

Meanwhile, the issue of some baby's daddy,
Of another plain Jew, marked through curved
Knives, gripped by inhabitants propositioning
Inappropriate places, gets regularly dismissed.

The courage, here, grows from rabbis' extra summons,
Those auger actions directed at solid challengers, bracing
Against persons attempting deleterious ordinances, our
Fighting truculent players & routing dilatory solutions.

Native scragginess means gainsaid goods
Won't muster past capital investments in life.
Local wisdom does surpass global influences.
Reflects. Deconstructs. Counters. Sieves. Saves.

Only to this spot, do the faithfuls' remains
Get transferred. Home's barren topographic
Beauty, its aconitum space, promises via
Golden sandstone facades, plus hard truths.

Lesser souls embrace geographic volatility
Excuse mundane rationalizing, selfish gains.
Abduct history, auction approbations. We
Jerusalemites look askance at those egregious.
We turn to G-d.

For Arlene: On Condition of a Smile and a Giggle

Abstemious children make pledges,
On condition of a smile and a giggle,
Particularly to groups of powerful
Individuals tending not to surface.

Given sunshine, also assorted conditions,
Plain folks' knowledge of astral energies
Can safeguard their entire communities,
Capably thwarting alien armies' coupes.

Understand, militants' muckles of wrapped cloths'
Flagged folds, absent creases, frees no fierce
Brothers or local lovelies, plus fails to presage
Inscrutability collected from the obstreperous.

The most dire cases of hostage taking pops eyes
Wide open, culls imperturbable affections, strikes,
Catalyzes the Stockholm Syndrome, suffers naught
After "merely" traumatizing isolated families.

Accordingly, when exhaling peppermint puffs,
Stretching to reach for hinted revelations, recall;
Keep all kemp and rimrock secured, brush both
Jaws twice daily. Plus, if protesting, write smarter.

Else, jackanapes will continue to make patent
Not-so-clandestine alliances with mercenaries.
See, embolden doggies sleep, chase no intruders.
As well, robust defense technologies can belly up.

When we love enough to die, to undergo whole
Tortures willingly, our cousins stop fashioning
Expiries. Even if permanently crippled, we'll
Live to travel to hope's more peaceful borders.

Lucana

An unfilled space or interval,
A gap of some six million, whose
Imperfect doss, void of even informal
Requiescats, sent telluric currents
Across history, stretched our global fingers.

Ishmael

The rationale behind Ishmael's continued existence remains beyond my ken.
Similarly, atomic collapses confuse administrations, especially when regimes balance
Power for power. Just as mystifying are cargo cults, poodles, lampshades,
Droopy basset hounds suffering from false pregnancies, the wearing of dhotis.

In war, as in peace, survivors ought not to suffer guilt, but to celebrate popcorn, silver, guns.
Nonetheless, understanding, like stratiform clouds, becomes cumulonimbus anvils,
Cirrus whispers, true stable atmosphere denizens, when logic's peritoneum is severed.

Equally unfathomable is children's gleaning of nutrition from artificial foods.
Foul origin is a fact, not a question. Vile destinies, too, bound beyond simple comprehension.
Malevolently nullified existence brings pain, forgets certainty. Satiation for pin pricks, lobsters,
Men, forms in laws, commandments, civil obedience, watery beds.
Otherwise, governments,
The media, and the public, respectively, derive their limits from improper decisions or stay away.

Perhaps, the truths of fragmented days, prejudice, broken homes, self-promotion, all prove,
How social insufficiency overcomes no soronous evil, or active calumny. Maybe
International accountability rests upon long-established desert patterns of avarice.
Possibly, like locusts, lice, plague-bearing rodents, wasteland adversaries linger by despoiling.

Clouds of Chicken Feathers

Clouds of chicken feathers float
Like summer snow on bitumen,
Meters before our windshields,
Teasing possibilities, including
Teleporting to regions, where
No terrorist or temperature
Inhibits any anodyne commute
Among school, work, home.

Desultory motoring, plus perfidious
Others, yet bring cultural collisions,
The likes of which, thereafter, seldom
Create cause for comfortable sharing.
Even persons, blessed to take early
Sabbath, fail at apotheoses involving
Children worn as shields, concrete
Tossed on lanes, random mad men.

Social lenticels need to offer better
Breathing, opportunities for walking
Away from ruins, improved survival
Rates. Some numbers need no proof;
Shoah's martyrs, fathers, mothers,
Babies, remain as in vitro warnings.
We light candles, thank The Almighty,
Dream, awake, empower Am Yisrael.

At present, comparable to Final Days,
Quiet denizens, alerted by alternate
Realities, stridently grasp antiquities;
Fiends' villages hold scant practical
Wisdom, little truth, humanity, peace.
Thus, potatoes, rocks, hens jumping
Off of pickups, justify overlooking
No depredations. We locals extirpate.

Throughout the Beginning of Social History

Throughout the beginning of social history,
Yaakov's sons distinguished here as holy.
The ways of prayer would cover all. No
Bashing, no exclusivity, no slurs; just unity.

Contemporary settlers' demographics, too,
Amass thinking, speaking, acting towards
Each other as balance against muddled facets,
Quantifiably garnering lives free from canards.

Honor, again and again, gleans conscience,
Behooves cleaving to forefathers' wisdoms,
Provides an ongoing purchase of miracles,
In local buildings glistening with sandstone.

Decebrate postures, those funky oppositions,
Faith improperly functioning, trendy rhetoric,
Disobedience to The Book, The Boss, Truth,
Omit vital spiritual nutrients, clinch iniquity.

When all of the nations turn against Israel,
Reflecting predawn eternity, we'll run, greet
Messiah's world without dressed up religion.
From the straits, we'll call upon The Name.

On the Road to Tsfat

On the road to Tsfat,
Toward grandchildren,
Maybe employment,
Some windy uncertainties,
Along with ethnic cows,
Random raptors, other thieves,
Pulled cars over to steal
Radishes, farming equipment,
Handheld electronic devices.

Nearby, foxes lay mashed
Like so much prison litter,
Smoking tobacco plus other
Weeds, themselves unwanted
Growths tumbleweeding
Through more humane settings
Civilizations, histories, diverse
Environments, reproducing quickly
Outside native habitats.

I think on assignments, dirty dishes,
Piles of waste in my kitchen fortress,
Galley proofs, signature pages,
Kilometers of negotiations.
Winter wheat's fresh green,
Clouds watch, without comment,
The people of legacy and their
Opponents. Verdant grace
Knows no membership.

The Jerusalem That Consumed Us

The Jerusalem that consumed
Leftovers from tourists dreaming,
When their bedchambers,
Sprayed against mosquitoes, or insurgents,
Overflowing

Floors carpeted with stone
Offer lucid moments, while
Courage sprung softly from tickets,
Valises, or concierges wheel holy
Hope,

By foot, by bus, not hired cab, locals transverse
The sky of endless sunshine.
Upstairs, a family belches out
A score of children,
Really.

Little hands shower heads with broken toys,
Projectiles made valuable because of speed
Whether doll heads,
Bent toothbrushes, or clothes pins
Drizzling,

Cold winter rains strangers
Together with pregnant women,
Whereas some fish mongers
Keep them floating,
Not gasping;

Chasmonaim's heroes, a quick excursion,
From expensive ancient hills' jaunt
For shekels, it's possible
To witness thousands years'
Whispering.

Donning Tallisims

Confusing religious symbols with laws,
Wearing icons, but not donning tallisims,
Means, ultimately, using selvedge to ornament.

Commentary on Aristotle, or on Tisias/Corax,
When wrung out by middle-aged moms,
Sings the wonders of gravitas hedgehogs.

Select departments' found materials craftsmen,
Like fathers returning from sugar caning,
Give the finger to civility's appurtenances.

Naïve fellows learn ways to deconstruct,
If speaking balderdash with university students.
Mimetic to a one, they generate cosmic tumult.

Some affirmative debaters miss, during cross-x,
Social seams joining voguing friends, elephant tusks,
Idolized triptychs, vacant bedrooms, winning lotteries.

Rubicons, east of The Missouri, bring
Timeshare tips to retired villagers wont to catch
Swinging caffeine-free artists' consciousness.

Recusal, maybe scholarships in photography,
Addiction, obdurate women, office music,
All remain accessible to teens and twenties.

Accordingly, working as a science writer
Continues on better than reviving twinned poems;
Tumid prose rarely attracts markets' evil luck.

Wedding *Birkat Hamazon* Again and Again

Dust, like Avraham *Avinu*'s,
Soaked from Angles,
Sheet the byways between the secular and *dati*
Whose joined steps, gather the manna
Transformed into mangoes and plums.

Charadi and *Masorti* both run before Shabbot.

My neighbor pours water, by buckets,
Down the community stairs.
His *Sfardi* home glistens such that only
The spiced chicken and the hot, seeded
Cakes best his welcome of *challot*.

Flickers plus light after sirens while local
Arabs amplify, using guns or loudspeakers.

Our minyon sings Carlebach.
Warm soups linger olfactory clues.
Black and white men return to lay hands
On children eying *parve* chocolate.
The first son is first blessed

Ima shines alongside her *vort*'s pearl drop.
Guests sing with Abba.
Windowsills smile flowers.

Outside, cats continue dumpster searches.
We walk, *Birchot Hamazon*, again and again.

Both the Instigator and her Mother

Both the instigator and her mother,
Showed their slight upon welcoming
That bride and groom into holy union.

Seems 'ol Green Eyes' pleasure made
Short shrift of fragile newlywed bliss;
Troublemaker had fallen for him first.

Later, the undertaker, who rowed the Styx
Accepted no shaggy dog tales, encouraged
Not one narration regarding unrequited love.

Shrugging, he whispered "time passes, clocks
Tick, life circles. Jealousy's rotten company.
Lassies ought to beseech higher places' help."

Ethnics Well Worth Their Weight in Things Charif

Ethnics well worth their weight in things charif,
Often opt for stills rather than contemporary video,
Prefer "seeming to" over intergenerational abilities.

For such, modern plumbing looks fairly attractive;
Hunkering down in light, single-wall tents, also
Overextending when hiking dunes, brings sweats.

Social norms viewed from behind computer screens,
Urges compassion for various odd acts, instills concern,
Raises charity for all sorts of urban warfare, terrorism.

Extorted governments, addicts sucking oil reserves,
Willingly endow NGOs, gift weapons, cash, bravado.
Temporalize responsibility for politic magnetization.

Neutralizing conflicting fields powers apart oppositions.
Legerdemain, related negotiations, means smoke, mirrors,
Ineptitude rewarding double-crossing and licentious foes.

I Don't Think I'd Like Being Dead

I don't think I'd like being dead,
Laying supine, my most private bits exposed to creepy crawlies,
Finding hedgehog friends defeated by meretrixes, those neither good nor fun
Verse mirrors chiming alongside of criminal rotational accelerations.

Woman who escape magicians' boxes of swords,
When faced with malevolent audiences, tend to kidnap their tormentors,
Rather than plod along inelegantly, buoyed by faith, shiny objects, the path of champions,
Seem more willingly buoyed by photographic memories of ordinary trollops.

Opening up truth, and then pushing out pus,
Becomes messy, can pong repetitions of olfactory möibus strips;
Acculturated sops, senescent beings, receptacles of irritations and elations,
Excuse demonizations, libels, other facets of war.

The temporarily Arab-occupied section of the Old City,
Gathers leaf mold for tinder, jerks metacarpal arches, sashays across media,
Fashions hard-won integrity into salutes to toughness, sass, hopeful rage,
Years after primary political diseases have been in remission.

Kindred arrangements for artificial flight,
Like purchased stimulation and other easy leisure,
Garner money for additional ammunition, maybe cigarettes, anvils, locust,
Forget apology, stuff formally uttered prayers, lets evil canter on.

Growth

And again I aspire,
To bring myself higher,
To wing away, set sail.
Anon, my dear dreams,
Restored, so it seems,
If ambition's fully derailed.

Evening's effervescent breeze,
Gifts sweet, simple liberties,
To beautifully plumed birds.
And grafts tight readers' words,
With pearly petal drops;
Pink, orange, probably white
Rots when realizing treasure's
Relative worth births pretend worlds,
Also dried blossoms as keepsake volumes

Yesterday, I pulled my pen across a page
Forsaken, even orphaned bits deigned
Fantastic things, brought along
Delicate imaginings;
Your likeness lay in fragile pieces

Long before they taught me how to catch a raven,
Watch a dolphin blue fish swimming blues,
Recall clouds, I learned that optimists are very busy souls
Deciding in which keys we sing our common grace.

Good talking in public needs good thinking in private
Educational elitism suits only the hegemony.

Dani and His Gun

Dani and his gun, dropped
Off at the local center,
To catch a van to the depot,
Where swarms of soldiers
Assemble, to get back
To base.

Those young men, all
Someone's sons, rifles
On shoulders, berets
Pinned firmly to shirts,
Gear rolled into duffels,
Wait patiently.

Snipers, other marksmen,
All someone's sons, aim,
Protect our holy land via
Hands, hearts, prayers,
Also bullets, grenades,
Rocket launchers.

On breaks, they bus home,
Slurp soup, chow on chicken,
Annoy sisters, hug parents,
Dandle nephews, nieces,
Crawl with small fry, forget
War for a while.

Our Quiet Reprisal

Yemin Moshe, near dawn,
Shared birthdays, weddings,
Alongside Sabbas and Savtas,
Among cedars, acacias, myrtle,
Oleaster, with renewed veneration
For all 613 mitzvot, conveys return.

The shuk, almost at breakfast time,
Where sipping, nibbling, frequenting
Dairy restaurants, grills, falafel stands,
Mended families, reacquainted strangers,
Pinchas' cold blooded execution of Zimri,
Cosbi, announces Torah's stanch resilience.

Nachalot, just 'bout any time of day,
Thru lively phizogs, bountiful middles,
Enveloped bending, swaying, otherwise
Praying, calling Father, hosting yeshiva
Boys, seminary girls, on Sabbaths, hagim,
All manner of future vows, joy links lineage.

The City of David, 'round high noon,
Eternal tapers, carefully articulated mots,
Blessings, infinite networks, G-d and man,
Man and man, doorposts and gates secured,
Protected, mezuzah-adorned, Shema-guarded,
Chushim's legacy, eliminates compeers of Esau.

The hills of Har Nof, exactly sunset,
Storefronts and shuls, wigged matrons,
Sticky children, soldiers enjoying leave,
Bustling gemachim: cars seats, medicines,
Food, linens, extra portions for widows, orphans,
Kallot, mentally indigent, well tends our new bonds.

This Holy City, throughout the night,
Hallel's urged b'tochen, Zechariah's Book
Of the Prophets, songs and visions of Moshiach,
We've completed mourning. The klal praises Hashem,
The Triumph of His kingdom, here, now, forevermore.
Golden limestone, holy people, divine plan, quiet reprisal.

Better a Lion's Tail

Better a lion's tail than a fox's head.
Jerusalem, all gilded quarters, holy radiance,
Gleams ancient perspective, His enduring love.

Friends' sma'achot, maybe shidduch dates,
Silently reify how Jews wed, quell advances,
Cling to light, not ill-advised behaviors, scandal.

Faithfulness marks Hebraic peace-making.
No amount of smiling, kvetching, tears, brings
Better fidelity, improved honor, greater splendor.

Smirks, hulls of hollowed pumpkins,
Perhaps hospitals' halls, mask no newly
Missing fingers, amputated feet, facial burns.

Global articulations distort authenticity.
Yom Hashoah's not universally recognized.
Stellar athletes, old hipsters, glitter draws crowds.

Mediated killing fields like LinkedIn, CNN bend
Fresh abeyance to wicked exposés. Traditional literary
Devices kowtow toward questionable pulses, social shadows.

Yet, concurrently, at the Kotel, night whispers true Torah
Joy, achdut's sweetness, mitzvots' perfume, service to Hashem.
Surpassing jasmine, honey, wine, good deeds reseal our covenant.

Blended Accounts

At Any Rate, Relationships

At any rate, relationships,
Art, can be deconstructed.

Rudiments of color, shape, texture,
Less so than conversations, govern.

Difficult pecuniary decisions,
Over which most spats occur,
Can elect indifferent discourse.

In striving to find light and air,
Among bleak towers, hunker
Down, hug proper rules.

Spiritual persons dwell as
Dear ones, most often.
Also, those allegedly
Wizened types act joyfully.

Those folk grant fewer spans
Of foul goings on; murder
Makes for summarized parts,
Maybe, additionally, disharmony.

Reassess components gleaned,
Plucked from lofty accolades.
Participate in frenetic moments.
Pull back wholly from discomfort,
Fill couplings with surmise.

Loud events provide only
Odd creations' secrets,
Manifesting weak qualities,
Better, kisses, forgetfulness,
Tutelage for the future.

Feuilletos

Newspaper supplements, doves, attached because
Clothing fragments, ritual baths, random scrolls,
Ancient budgets, also babies, fail when struggling;
Cohorts ought to include instructions for the dying.

Evidence littermates' truce over trenchant brothers.
Consider, too, money makers' surprises, sometimes
Bound forward from conglomerated efforts, toast,
Successfully cloning, matchy hairdos, fournagieres.

Salacious talk, backyard dissonance, especially sorts
Endured by pompom girls' collective friendliness, lags,
In a manner of speaking, depends on tulips, amorettis,
Fence posts surrounding homesteads, strays' fidelity.

When sitting near chilled, occupied perambulators,
Hedgehogs regard warring siblings with disdain.
Obligatory Carlebach music, among new guitarists,
Slides boas freely over urban straits, under gutters.

Besides, the moment when kin audaciously quit,
We tend to lauder over the narcoleptics among us.
It would be better to take only memories, thank
Your waiters, remember to pay all bills on time.

Death Sentence

Today, I wait death sentence.
Excuses, accounts, even boldness. if embellished, ebbs.
To wit, tomorrow's fancy remains embroidered,
Endorsed as such a day as when roiling warnings
Will roll against shores yielding no better truth,
No greater stone than pathetic children's viscera.

We sorrow for want of more lucid imaginings
Before returning to elevate our dregs.
Life's complications, impediments, crucial continuities
Sit strictly in boxes belonging to generations, maybe leaders,
Certainly to "civilian obligations," sans glitz or not,
Also, folded as existential minutia of social currency.

Only fairy tales, kiddie pabulum, other nonsense
Hold hoary brutality as accountability-free;
In thinking women's castles, heads of state
Unabashedly redefine select commonplaces
Confabulating laws again and once more until
The cock crows, dawn or not, with measured righteousness.

The Goody-Goody People

The goody-goody people depend on friends for personal profligacy;
Their highest form of personal gratification functions like a baby's dummy,
Substitutes when vainglorious folk must, perforce, find means to obdurate,
In the company of captains, corporals, divas, bluebloods, or other military sorts.
Consider that assistant bank managers are known for their ostentatious ways.

Of course, slung mud not only decorates, but heals, as well.
Hard tests, made paltry, eventually evolve into comestibles suitable for sustenance,
During spans when critters surface, stick slick tongues to the air, sneeze.
Winning ways, good desiccants all, help preserve food, fame, faded notions,
Plus personal glory, false eyelash clumps, toe glitter, even as pernicious
beasts thrive.

It seems that while perfection remains underrated, overpaid, possibly trumped,
Unless Kingdom Come advises us against doing business with parlous louts,
Perdition scares few among the gold-diggers, politicians, scholarship seekers,
Beauty parlor entrepreneurs, or tennis instructors. After all, apostasy's no siren;
The greater populace prefers to engage in prurient acts and refuses toothbrushes.

At best, hoards might be shuttled toward gaping maws to stuff full those orifices.
Sure, there's little taste in officious hedge fund mongers, industrial tycoons,
other thieves.
But officious clerks, too, give the heave ho whenever their peripatetic assemblages,
Cause suffering among citizens, in saloons, at rave parties, maybe behind
schoolyards.
Anarchy's clarion's silenced. Plenty of tocsins stay around to clean up business.

Amid Giants' Awkward Works

Our portion of creation, humanity,
Still insouciantly harbors, shelters
Mercator projections of fey reality.

Few dead, whether in spirit, or in fact,
Improve cumulative averages fainting.
Rather, denizens code exposed to ice.
Survivors cost unnatural bride prices
Still, make no noise near sheep drops.

Consider, a recent assignment involving cassowaries,
Also fossas found among small numbers of couples,
By dint of sacrificing academic poutines, solenodons.
After shuffle board failed, we kicked in local cuisine.

Departed people helped stumbling emotions link up.
Counterpoint to teaching Boston's advanced glazing,
They shock mission-driven food beasts' appreciation,
Hire substitutes for high profile social roles & nostrils.
When driving landaus, cuddling industry norms, most
People come alive, count amid giants' awkward works.

So, I Appreciate Brakes

So, I appreciate brakes, which work. Always.
Also, enough toilet paper to get through the night.
Finding my spectacles, likewise, rates as "needed"
As does tea in the morning, plus seltzer for lunch.

A day empty of phone messaging, too, brings cheer.
Having sufficient hours of sleep, regular showers,
Hot food, comforts me, plunks my life in working order.
Equally, I'm glad when I can manage time at the gym.

"Worth" ain't restricted to dollars, euros, yen.
Neither is quality's texture measured by fashion.
More exactly, goodness' properties most often arrive
Upon easing away from irritations, troubles, or woes.

Rusty Memories: Home for the Holidays

Twinkle, twinkle, dither, doo,
Sleigh bells, bad smells, naked you.

Menacing, mincing, pinching poo,
Ornaments and pine trees, too.

Drop cloth, litter, recurring fright,
Cat scoffed birds all this twelfth night.

Bighted , shattered, broken much,
Crippled from unwanted touch.

Joy, hope, faith have run away,
Found safer shadows for this day.

He Upbraids his Wife

He upbraids his wife, hates her self-conceit.
Most often, though, in nuzzling her neck,
The Man's deaf to her trumpeted sacrifices.

Their daily chaos, all dirty laundry, smudged
Kisses, revived hurts, broken pots, other bits,
Remain unremarkable in proffering protection.

Belated rewards for more perilous paths stall,
Take into consideration no displaced music,
Ignore all other martial-associated privileges.

Depravation pushes intimacy on such beloveds.
They rush, finally, not the highest flowering,
Barely perceivable, their union's ruined blossoms.

Thereafter, often sun spaces before nightfall,
When words, like winter's forest leaves,
Grow brittle, his eyes sparkle blue-white.

He reflects military strongholds' treasures, recalls
Fortress schools and nunneries, buried for eras.
No chairman of the board or like henchmen win.

Covered with silver, antiquated feelings surface,
She examines the notion that it's best to observe
Partners when they're deeply sleeping or dead.

Initially Thrilled to the Idea of Memories

We initially thrilled to the idea of memories, all snowflake-shaped,
Best explained visa via underpaid heroines, corn flakes, cow patties.

Owned anxieties attached to hurting children, though, made for thin soup,
Created portions of limited serenity, concealed life's verities, urged
stumbling upon.

In the bedrooms of critical thinkers, the lowest sort of games received our
revisions,
Long bits get broadcast got published. We preempted guesses, threw stones
at crows.

No harm came from our country club manners, fish eyes, pickled calf feet,
puppy ears,
Overpriced patisseries, trepanning avuncular persons, belching loudly in
public, cursing.

Believing war's sheathed swords could cancel duels, disappear acne, we
banished
Truth-bearing insights contingent on the province of hedgehogs and small,
white ducks.

Online Housewife Evaluations

She was able to fly away and land in the midst of interpersonal negotiations,
Those sorts of bits that embrace good character, but mix "safe" behaviors
with gasoline,
Never calming down after her online housewife evaluations got forwarded.

Replies to queries about her presence of mind, public relations sites, other
nonsense,
Also, traditional approaches to dusting, hiking in the woods, documenting
burnt cake failed;
So many pocketed cell phones got gnawed on by her Aussie Doodle dog.

Considering that rethinking carpool strategies, corporate takeovers, plus
grocery lists,
Couldn't bring her children home earlier, conquer government interns,
make short work of baking,
Her taxes, especially those forms squiggled during colic-filled night, shriveled.

Just as every unmopped droplet of grime became, too quickly, so much
extra laundry,
Her "employer's" suggestions, demands from a fellow ousted for insider
trading, theft, fraud,
Made wonky any residual findings provided by media crews, detectives,
associates.

His buddies continued to insist that no woman above the age of menses
should pout,
That wives never need include peaceniks, domestic divas coteries, tea parties
experts in their hours,
But the universal propensity for equipment maintenance won.

In brief, rent suited when it came to overnight trysts. Purchase power, however,
Remains preferable for carnal acts filed as permanent byways and marked
by decisiveness.
The departing matron smiled weakly, while tracking flour through the back door.

Employing Muster when Sending Extra Emails

Shoving him in the head caused a complete absence of redeeming qualities
Ordinarily common to main-belt asteroid minors encapsulating their
experiences.
Consequently, he lost completely, any regard: for cancer survivors who die,
suddenly,
From complications of pneumonia, for altruistic bouquets, and for fallen
blossoms.

Elsewhere, a mom who sacrificed political accomplishments to devote herself
to children,
Witnessed their visceral-intense mutilation under the wheels of an utterly
drunk driver.
Kismet spins not only the goings on of space station occupants, but also of
labor leaders.
(Domestic drudgery remains no guaranteed retreat from reelection promises
or pain).

Clerks muster courage when sending extra emails about professional
interfaces;
Ancient environs, their days and nights reputed to be intensely precious, elicit,
Over millennia, patterns of social responses deemed unreasonable elsewhere.
Internal exploration, only sometimes, is easier to understand than
metamorphosis.

Know that olive oil's still scarce, teacher-parent conference can't be
rescheduled,
Little portions of goodness, fortuitous results, ill-perceived notions of nature,
Spin against long spans of general happiness, also, "attitude" mentioned twice,
Old-fashioned tendencies try to improve character traits able to instill deeds
of kindness.

Seemingly inconsequentially large numbers of people embrace wee cases of
extortion.
The populous attributes no little importance to the support teams that
hold them up.
Alternatively, mobs soldier against steel structures, wooden tracks, cheap
plastic, glass,
Fashion weddings, affairs, educations, compete against moon bases for quality
adventure.

Rhetorically-manufactured world news, insidiously persists in tinting
our experiences,
On condition of receiving gifts like high tower residencies, operation
center visits,
Our kowtowing to superiors, catching squirrels for breakfast, sniffing
them, eating them.
Alternatively, it's ignorant sorts who cause the blocks by which we
proletariats stumble.

Psychological Trials

None of the late day spies were possessed with more than loyalty to handlers,
Until such thoughts made the rounds of bars, parked cars, drug dens, coffee shops.

One mighty example of espionage missed, altogether, the perspective of mothers,
Who regard teenagers as lingering liabilities, chow hounds, sources of domestic
entropy.

Coupling clandestinely in a government apartment meant going AWOL,
Rejecting assignments, spoofing mentors, turning backs, paying hazard prices.

If only academic fervor might drive pawns like him toward collection points,
She would have had merely to ask for course corrections, without safeties.

Nonetheless, "helping restore political balance" brought along bikinied dividends,
Economic stimulus packages, disproportional amounts of bribes, buried treasure,
laughs.

His Renewed Acquaintance

His renewed acquaintance,
That winsome buddy boy,
Important enough to expedite
Meat or cheese across deli lines,
Coughed, stumbled, and then fell dead.

Otherwise happy in his middle class home,
Such a fellow revealed, at time of autopsy,
Some of his creative furries notwithstanding,
Patterns of investments in angel networks
(Certain URLs were inked on his skin).

His widow declared it's better to teach raw ceramics,
Hike for empties, rescue tourists, photograph Mt. Everest,
Jumble fiduciary directives, streak at awards ceremonies,
Research skinks, hide homework, pursue dunderdoodles,
Than keel over when eating pastrami on rye, with pickles.

No purple towel magic or blue lagoon wishes save
From lethal ineptitude, unspecified hopelessness;
Consider, mostly aggressive business practices,
Parachute souls away, bring heart break, seizures,
Angina spelled out via letters of tax loopholes.

Accordingly, various ways of crumbling crackers,
Mushrooming middles plus Zen retreats aside,
Call up mange rivers to join commonplace lives
Until peace makers' pace makers tick remorse,
Bind material goods against breathing's relative worth.

Caught Muskrats

Muskrats, caught in traps, continue to make a difference, at shekels per day.
Bank accounts, simultaneously hiding intestines, though, resolve no
conundrums.
Private rooms, also circles' memberships, might or not prove beyond that realm.

Whenever being helped up a building's front steps, one ought to curtsey.
Simply, discovered ruses tend to send multiple emails to outworlder
patrons.
Self-reflective moments, alternatively, become privy to most live thoughts.

Plus, following residential questions makes for sieved agencies, lost sheep farts.
Choice gets implicitly taught by explicated moments more than odd
circumstances;
Unresolved responses notwithstanding, nearly all minor league pitchers
strike out.

Should you desire to expose condemnatory feelings, not only will birdsong fail,
But, additionally, homeless teenagers will, after a manner, act in kind. Great
fireballs
Blaze first in upper atmospheres, then, only later, drift across continents.

Assistance with Quickly Becoming Unbearable

Admittedly more influenced by remonstrance than valor, no longer interested
In middle aged men's rhetorical scrutiny, or payola,
That snip of a gal gleaned endorphin-driven support.

Her near daily cross-examinations yielded chicken coop-level amounts of excitement,
Brought happiness, renal center remittances, sobriety,
Except when she refused to return our missing goldfish.

Thereafter, friends, meaning to finesse a little blackmail as a neighborly offering,
Evaporated, never to be seen among balding babies born after 1950.
Changes in Massachusetts' legislature suddenly almost made sense.

Still, the sight of the reptiles, of stuffed animals, of overwrought teenagers, repelled her,
Sending associated hand maidens back for psychology studies, chemistry labs, math.
Select individuals, within the academy, blamed the inoculation theory of persuasion.

Rock is Home

Rock is home. Stone's sound, verifiable, secure.
Steadfastly warms, holds light and heat until
Street crews sweep up odd gender-defined litter.
Then, we go home hungry, contemplate necessities.

Compassion lifts up. Empathy elevates, promotes, raises.
Coexists with neighbors, makes grandchildren sing unless
Green grocer bribe police, other bureaucrats.
Thereafter, we might miscalculate tearing motions.

Today's common denominators rot. Oversimplification hurts,
punctures, destroys.
Depletes denizen quirkiness, denudes half- life love pending times when
Pursuing aggressors halt growth's utility.
From then on, we scrutinize each other's laundry.

Setting aside taxes harms. Levies spoil, impair, otherwise sting.
Collects fumbling more than friendship, mars anticipating
happenstances where
Formal discourse serves disproportionate directives.
Subsequently, our obligation to tolerance fades.

Writing proceeds accordingly. Words reflect influence, authority, weight.
Heal slowly the confluence of money, power, greed, save for instances
including
Internet machinations hatching varied qualities of charm.
Later, we embrace evil, throw out moral strictures.

A June Full of Cherries

Piquant, yet tender, portrayals of festivities' "field kitchens"
Forgive lapses such as young beasties, insufficiently protected points of view,
Great accidents of interest, the merged foci of welcoming, disbanding, hugging,
Also dressing in gold spandex, belly dancing, weaving baskets, noting
What's working for whom, and why, tasting, maybe teasing,
Playing with prefixes, acting wonky, listening to exclamations,
Plus skipping along peripheral places makes for forgetting staid rubrics.

When sloughing worldly woes, celebrating significant events,
Consuming even minute mounds of funky antimeria, during alternate decades,
It's possible to categorize material goods, let alone affective states, tayras,
Human relationships (patterned both tacit and affective), trilobites, glabrous birds,
As belonging to solid-hoofed herbivorous quadruped or other vehicles' barns
Meant to entertain visa via ornaments, food, drink, actualized space, vessels,
Likewise the compelled restoration of pumpkin crowns or thornbushes, works.

Other times, those of mind-muddle mode, find it difficult to regard
Disruptions amicably, to smile, to say nothing, or, perhaps, to interact quietly,
Guest in pediatric wards, receive mistaken attributions causality,
Get elected because of money or connections, override baser inclinations,
Ignore global societies, local neighborhoods, and familial conundrums,
Combine behavioral modifications for purposes of suck, grandeur, climate,
Additionally, post publishers' letters on refrigerators, all while spinning in circles.

Most often, though, cats lull innocently, whereas hounds snore, worms whistle,
Chickadee ringleaders and Komodo dragon catalysts glibly forecast entire
Epics for good findings, comradely inspiration, and conceptualized work.
Burnt toast, bitter coffee, broken eggs, too, make for playful family times,
Distinct units of innocent, mentalists' gymnastics, deadly mustelids, plus pungent
Cycles of socks, big skirts, small spices, deflected ants, termites, and do-gooders.
Alternatively, in June, bowls full of cherries get agitated. A mom can dream.

Fish Grill

Certain loathsome moves do not deter some wolves from baying.
    Remarkable   dissolved peduncles   droop,
Weighed down by too many bursts of flowers. Suddenly sessile,
    Plants   personify   entire generations.
Apathetic responses from a White House, numb to Mideast woes,
    Embrace   dunes   as middens.
The rest of us get stuck perusing global dumps for all manners
    Irrational   diplomatic   hypnagogic.
Just saying, most munge, especially birthed from old NSA spins,
    Makes kings   oil barons   tyrants.
After all, what's friends when rivals readily supply our renown?

Eating Peas

Eating peas,
Like popping bubble wrap,
Most often, regardless of school,
Obscures chitchat, fantasy play, kin.

Kissing frogs,
Getting work into print,
Making snide remarks, offsets
Responsibilities to book publishers.

Eschewing notions,
Perhaps, brings about science,
Meant, decades ago, to sort out
Differences of zonkeys, zebroids, okapis.

Taking up basket weaving,
Mirroring The Big Island's vogue,
In semantics, rhetoric, ethics, pedagogy,
Banishes potential commonplaces, outsells recognition.

Flapping discourse,
Substituting for functional kitchens,
Temporarily grants welcome to negotiated insights
Bring forward ministrations focused on siblings, cousins, dogs.

Generating words,
Ghostwriting sociology or psychology texts,
In spits of small numbers meant for outsourcing,
Kindly predisposes some aliens, standardized patients, doves.

Accommodating random realities,
Easing dreamy expressions breath by breath,
Making eschewed poetry explode, dance the rumba,
Causes truth to stumble into arabesques, improved turnout.

Fruit Loops Are Never Enough

Fruit loops are never enough to satisfy.
Likewise, malabi leaves social strata wanting.
Blowing kisses binds attention, secures wills.
Where oboes chant, cattails won't grow.

No ebullient child paints on small smiles.
Asking parents to remove jumbotrons, or
Leave glossies behind at checkout lines,
Makes for lapsed, mawkish moments.

As well, cultural phenoms regularly impress
By changing Facebook status.
East of Eden, Jarls, chieftains, other natives,
Thumb young entrepreneurs' body parts.

Wendigos, chimeras, also imaginary lions
Roar when listserve-using writers aid,
Offline, data hunting and gathering.
Eidetic memories ought not use algae-frothing.

Meaningful sock fibers, ketchup recipes,
Acrylic paint, maybe seatbelts, equally,
Sequence heartsong with prosaic lyrics,
Bring table sacrifices, senior proms, pumpkins.

One thousand suicidal monkeys, all dogma potion,
Establish rationales for hiding enemies, excavate
Small bits, gawk mercenaries, crows, clairvoyants,
Keep on pouring milk over sugared cereal.

Conclusion:
The Three Dimensions of Decision-Making

Guarding civilization's ethics used to mean
Stuffing vassals with nutritious misdirection.

These days, though, hirsute rhetoric namely involves
Volleying emails, IMs, also links to websites.
No longer do the horrific nature of seditious clerks, nor
The wonder concomitant to building new highways, inspire.

Long after hydration, some denizens, even so,
Continue along with moral fecklessness,
Pretending that their economic language capably brings
Dialogical carminatives to play (they dismiss gas).
Sadly, among hedgehogs, assistant bank managers, their friends,
Ululations most often send critters into bestial spasms.

With greater understanding than is found
In comic books, software manuals, maybe tax forms,
Noble messengers could, foreseeably, make palpable
The excoriation of slick foils. However, economic jingoism
Makes ghosts out of towns, barnyard animals, plus regular folk,
Causes moral dandies to spout beyond goldfish, forces
Leadership to: sing along with suggested, invective discourse,
Abscond virtue, and hide their visages in the ranks of shunpikers.

Accordingly, homemakers remain advised to filling
Their attitudes, values, larders with the spicy remains
Of the three dimensions of decision-making, all of which
Were known to be formerly issued by the mass media.
Multigenerational get-togethers might offer up apple pie,
Perimenopausal hootennies, plated farro, intergenerational resistance.
Yet, despite shared watermelon, cucumbers, squash,
The University of Corn's lessons notwithstanding,
At boss' behest, citizens parley fraudulent articulations into promises,
Bundle reality for the rag factory, shrug at flickering veracities.

Acknowledgments

Admittedly more influenced by my contemporaries than by my prickle of imaginary hedgehogs, I remain indebted to certain editors who have published my books of poetry, who have accepted atypically large amounts of my individual poems, or who have encouraged me to fashion yet more poetic works. I thank: Don Webb and Bill Bowler of *Bewildering Stories*, Sarah Kahn of *BRICKrhetoric*, Adam Henry Carrière of *Danse Macabre*, MH Clay and Johnny Olson of *Mad Swirl*, Zvi A. Sesling of *Muddy River Poetry Review*, Rick Lupert of *Poetry Super Highway*, Beth Adams and Dave Bonta of *Qarrtsiluni*, Kelly Hartog of *Scribblers on the Roof*, Amy Souza of *Spark!*, Rupert Loydell of *Stride Magazine*, Russell Streur of *The Camel Saloon* and of The Camel Saloon Books on Blog, David Whitehouse of *The Lesser Flamingo*, Daniel E. Levenson of *The New Vilna Review*, Pamela Tyree Griffin of *The Shine Journal* and of *Joyful!*, Annmarie Lockhart of *vox poetica* and of Unbound CONTENT, and David A. Pick of *Winamop*.

Similarly, I will always be indebted to Sorah Rosenblatt, of blessed memory. As well, my husband, my sons, and my daughters continue to: challenge my perspectives, inspire me to exclaim over life's minutiae, and, most importantly, to remember that my writing ought to remain just one among the many factors of my life. My dear ones simultaneously elevate and anchor me.

Credits

"A June Full of Cherries." *Mad Swirl*. Sep. 2012. Rpt. *The Little Temple of My Sleeping Bag*. Dancing Girl Press. Sep. 2014.

"Accounts Due: Reckoning with Trauma." *Primalzine*. Apr. 2012.

"All of the Wisdom that is a Grey Cat's: An Early Morning Soliloquy." *Muddy River Poetry Review*. Nov. 2010.

"All Those Nooks and Crannies." *vox poetica*. Nov. 2012.

"Alphabetical Trails." *Poetry Super Highway*. Nov. 2008.

"Alternate Childcare Providers Can't Feel Compelled." *Ken*Again*. Dec. 2014.

"Amid Giants' Awkward Words." *Winamop*. Apr. 2014.

"Among Seaweed." *The Lesser Flamingo*. May 2009.

"Another Dead Goldfish." *Danse Macabre*. July 2012.

"Assistance with Quickly Becoming Unbearable." *Really System*. Apr. 2014. Rpt. in the short story "Assistance with Quickly Becoming Unbearable." *Bewildering Stories*. Aug. 2014.

"At Any Rate, Relationships." *Fowl Feather Review*. Feb. 2015.

"Autumn Migration." *The Shine Journal*. Mar. 2011.

"Baby Spits Peas." *Poetry Super Highway*. Nov. 2008.

"Baby's Friends." *vox poetica*. Apr. 2010.

"Better a Lion's Tail" as "Considerations for Yom Hoashoah: Better a Lion's Tail." *Poetry Super Highway*. Yom Hashoah Issue. Apr. 2013.

"Bird Wonder." *Word Catalyst*. Nov. 2009.

"Both the Investigator and Her Mother." *Spark!* Jun. 2014.

"But Loving You." *BRICKrhetoric*. Aug. 2012. 27-28.

"Caught Muskrats." *Bewildering Stories*. Sep. 2014.

"Changes in Field Experiments." *BRICKrhetoric*. Feb. 2012.

"Closed Caskets and Bullfinches." *Ol' Chanty*. Jun. 2014

"Clouds of Chicken Feathers." *The Voices Project*. Aug. 2014.

"Cricket." *Word Catalyst*. Nov. 2009.

"Daddy's Ankle Biters' Extravagance." *The Lesser Flamingo*. Nov. 2009.

"Dani and His Gun." *Winamop*. Sep. 2015.

"Day-old Cakes." *The Camel Saloon*. Jul. 2012.

"Dear Tablet (A Requiem by a Seventh Grader)." *Winamop*. Oct. 2011.

"Death Sentence." *The Camel Saloon*. Jul. 2011.

"Donning Tallisims." *The Camel Saloon*. Aug. 2013.

"Eating Peas." *Mad Swirl*. Oct. 2013. Rpt. *Dancing with Hedgehogs*. Fowlpox Press. Dec. 2014.

"Education before Marrige." *vox poetica*. Jul. 2013.

"Employing Muster when Sending Extra Emails." *Ygdrasil*. Sep. 2013.

"Empty of Meaningful Intelligence," *BRICkrhetoric*. Nov. 2011.

"Envied Like so Many Flamingos Missing Carotenoid." *The Camel Saloon*. Nov. 2014.

"Even Linda Ronstadt Grew a Chin." *Danse Macabre*. Dec. 2012.

"Even the Rainbow Tank's Fish Saluted." *The Camel Saloon*. Jun. 2014.

"Exposition's Heart-felt Blushes (an *Awdl Gywydd*)." *Winamop*. Dec. 2012.

"Feuilletos." *Ken*Again*. Dec. 2014.

"Fish Grill." *Dancing with Hedgehogs*. Fowlpox Press. Dec. 2014.

"For Arlene: On Condition of a Smile and a Giggle." *Mad Swirl*. Nov. 2014.

"For Ezra: Familial Wishes for a New Nighttime Traveler." *Mastodon Dentist*. Oct. 2009. 25.

"Forbs be Blessed." *Winamop*. Dec. 2014.

"Friendship." *The Cat's Meow*. Jul. 2011.

"Frozen Green Beans on Your Face." *Mad Swirl*. May 2012.

"Fruit Loops are never Enough." *Every Day Poems*. Oct. 2013. Rpt. *The Little Temple of My Sleeping Bag*. Dancing Girl Press. Sep. 2014.

"Gentle Spray." *Poetry Breakfast*. Jan. 2012.

"Germane Adolescents." *BRICkrhetoric*. Aug. 2012. 27-28.

"Growth." *Winamop*. Mar. 2103. Rpt. *The Little Temple of My Sleeping Bag*. Dancing Girl Press. Sep. 2014.

"Halfway to Naked." *The Camel Saloon*. Dec. 2011.

"Harmony's Third Chord (*a Casbairdne*)." *BRICKrhetoric*. Dec. 2012.

"Hatched Loved Ones." *Literary Hatchet*. May 2013.

"He Upbraids his Wife." *Bewildering Stories*. Feb. 2015.

"Heart-felt Festival." *The Camel Saloon*. Sep. 2011.

"Heart's Preamble." *Winamop*. Mar. 2013.

"Hip Hop Music among the Branches." *Spark!* Feb. 2014. Rpt. *Dancing with Hedgehogs*. Fowlpox Press. Dec. 2014.

"His Renewed Acquaintance." *Ygdrasil*. Sep. 2013.

"Holidays' Fallibility." *Danse Macabre*. Nov. 2011.

"How the Next Generation Succumbed to the End of Morality." *The Camel Saloon*. Nov. 2011.

"I Don't Think I'd Like Being Dead." *Dancing with Hedgehogs*. Fowlpox Press. Dec. 2014.

"If You Need a Reason to Read under the Covers." *vox poetica*. Feb. 2015.

"Infatuation, More Honestly." *vox poetica*. Jun. 2013. Rpt. *The Little Temple of My Sleeping Bag*. Dancing Girl Press. Sep. 2014.

"Initially Thrilled to the Idea of Memories." *Really System*. Oct. 2014.

"Ishmael." *Haggard and Halloo*. Sep. 2012.

"It's not about the Sex." *The Camel Saloon*. Feb. 2013. Rpt. *The Little Temple of My Sleeping Bag*. Dancing Girl Press. Sep. 2014.

"Jukebox Jury." *vox poetica*. Apr. 2012.

"Keeping Imaginary Hedgehogs Trim via Liberal Politics." *Mad Swirl*. Jun. 2011.

"Like is Because." *Verse Wisconsin*. Oct. 2013.

"Lucana." *The Camel Saloon*. Mar. 2012.

"Mirage." *The Cat's Meow*. Jul. 2011

"My Daughter Bangs Pot Lids" as "My Baby Bangs Pot Lids." *The Cat's Meow*. Jul. 2011."

"Natural Balance." *Literary Mama*. Nov. 2008.

"Natural Progressions." *Pinkeyelemonade*. Feb. 2012.

"Not Entirely Becoming Grandma." *vox poetica*. Nov. 2012.

"Not of Small Value." *Tipton Poetry Review*. Mar. 2012. 31.

"Not Partial to the Purple Falcon." *Bewildering Stories*. Jan. 2015.

"Nutritional Inconveniences." *Mom Writers Literary Magazine*. May 2009. 73.

"Ode to Aerosols." *The Lesser Flamingo*. Jun. 2009.

"Older Girls Ought Not, as Spinsters." *BRICKrhetoric*. Feb. 2012.

"On the Road to Tsfat." *Spark!* Feb. 2015.

"One Minute Before Salvation: Yom Hazikaron before Yom Ha'atzmaut." *Penny Ante Feud*. Aug. 2011.

"Online Housewife Evaluations." *BRICKrhetoric*. Jun. 2014.

"Only after Dosing on Vicodin." *Bewildering Stories*. Jan. 2015.

"Our Quiet Reprisal." *Poetry Super Highway*. Yom Hashoah Issue. Apr. 2014.

"Parenting's Saxophone Smiles." *Spark!* Feb. 1012.

"Peaches Merit." *Poetry Breakfast*. May 2012.

"Permutations which Transform." *Mad Swirl*. Sep. 2011.

"Pillow Talk's Expediency." *Bewildering Stories*. Jun. 2013.

"Plastic Surgery." *The Camel Saloon*. Aug. 2012.

"Poplar." *The Cat's Meow*. Jul. 2011.

"Psychological Trials." *The Camel Saloon*. Sep. 2014.

"Quaternary Glaciation in the American Midwest." *The Camel Saloon*. Apr. 2013.

"Redirecting Hurt." *Visceral Uterus*. May 2013.

"Rock is Home." *Ygdrasil*. May 2013.

"Rusty Memories." *Danse Macabre*. Aug. 2012.

"Simple Miracles." *Word Catalyst*. Nov. 2009.

"So, I Appreciate Brakes." *Winamop*. Jul. 2014.

"Social Evolution." *Danse Macabre*. Aug. 2011.

"Song of Oenomelian." *Joyful!* Sept. 2008.

"Sylvan Song." *Winamop*. Jan. 2012.

"Taking Apart a Pixie." *Haggard and Halloo.* Jan. 2012.

"The ABCs of Emotional Suicide." *Winamop.* Nov. 2014.

"The Effect of Cumin on Mankind Can't Replace Pop-Pop." *Litsnack.* Mar. 2011.

"The Goody-Goody People." *Bewildering Stories.* Oct. 2014.

"The Jerusalem that Consumed Us." *Language and Culture Magazine.* Summer/Fall 2009.

"The Three Dimensions of Decision-Making." *vox poetica.* Nov. 2012.

"The Unsustainability of Bugs Tracking Breadcrumbs." *Mad Swirl.* Sep. 2014.

"The Warrior's Mother." *Mad Swirl.* Apr. 2013.

"The Zebra Hoof Beats of Buttercup Boys." *The Mother Magazine.* Jul. /Aug. 2009. 41.

"Then the Wind." *Social-i Magazine.* Dec. 2010. 7.

"There's a Seam." *The Mother Magazine.* Mar. /Apr. 2009. 40.

"Throughout the Beginning of Social History." *The Camel Saloon.* Jun. 2014.

"Twined, We Two, Tenderly." *Winamop.* May 2012.

"Vitreous Recollections: That Summer's Glaze." Spark! Sep. 2010.

"Until Exhausted." *Spark!* Jun. 2014.

"Watching Raindrops Dance." *Unfettered Verse.* Dec. 2008.

"Wedding Birkat Hamazon" as "Birkat Hamazon Again and Again." Supernal Factors. *Camel Saloon.* Books on Blog. Aug. 2012.

"Windfall Fruit." *Spark!* May 2011.

"Your Hushed, Stealthy Looks." *The Camel Saloon.* Jun. 2012.

"Your Warm Stomach." *The Muddy River Poetry Review.* May 2012.

About the Author

Photograph by: Yiftach Paltrowitz

KJ Hannah Greenberg's whimsical writing buds in pastures where gelatinous wildebeests roam and beneath the soil where fey hedgehogs play. She's been nominated four times for the Pushcart Prize in Literature, and once for The Best of the Net.

Hannah's short story collections are: *Concatenation: A Compendium* (Bards & Sages Publishing, 2017), *Can I be Rare, Too?* (Bards & Sages Publishing, 2017), *Friends and Rabid Hedgehogs* (Bards & Sages Publishing, 2016), *Cryptids* (Bards & Sages Publishing, 2015), *The Immediacy of Emotional Kerfuffles,* 2nd ed. (Bards and Sages Publishing, 2015), and *Don't Pet the Sweaty Things,* 2nd ed. (Bards and Sages Publishing, 2014). Her musical is *Watercolors* (Scotch & Soda Productions, 1979).

Hannah's nonfiction books are: *Word Citizen: Uncommon Thoughts on Writing, Motherhood & Life in Jerusalem* (Tailwinds Press, 2015), *Jerusalem Sunrise* (Imago Press, 2015), *Oblivious to the Obvious: Wishfully Mindful Parenting* (French Creek Press, 2010), and *Conversations on Communication Ethics* (Praeger, 1991).

Hannah's poetry books are: *A Grand Sociology Lesson* (Lit Fest Press, 2016), *Dancing with Hedgehogs,* (Fowlpox Press, 2014), *The Little Temple of My Sleeping Bag* (Dancing Girl Press, 2014), *Citrus-Inspired Ceramics* (Aldrich Press, 2013), *Intelligence's Vast Bonfires* (Lazarus Media, 2012), *Supernal Factors* (The Camel Saloon Books on Blog, 2012), *Fluid & Crystallized* (Fowlpox Press, 2012), and *A Bank Robber's Bad Luck with His Ex-Girlfriend* (Unbound CONTENT, 2011).

Selected Titles Published by Unbound Content